Everlasting Light

Lily K. Lewis

WESTBOW
PRESS®
A DIVISION OF THOMAS NELSON
& ZONDERVAN

WestBow Press books may be ordered through booksellers or by contacting:

WestBow Press
A Division of Thomas Nelson & Zondervan
1663 Liberty Drive
Bloomington, IN 47403
www.westbowpress.com
844-714-3454

ISBN: 978-1-6642-6323-9 (sc)
ISBN: 978-1-6642-6324-6 (hc)
ISBN: 978-1-6642-6322-2 (e)

Library of Congress Control Number: 2022906593

Print information available on the last page.

WestBow Press rev. date: 04/25/2022

Note from the Author

Every name mentioned in this book was used with direct
permission from each person. I hope you enjoy this book and that
it helps you see God's everlasting light a little more clearly.

Wishing you much love and light, Lily K. Lewis

To my aunt and uncle, Matt and Jeannie, for giving me the opportunity to be a light, and to my God, Who has carried me through so much and brought me out stronger: I thank You with all my heart, soul, and strength. You are my Everything.

Contents

The Light that Never Fades

Unbreakable Joy 1

The Father of Lights 6

Fireflies 9

Chasing Sunsets and Seeking the Lord 14

Treasure 18

The Message That Continues Forever 23

God Will Provide the Words 27

Perspective 30

Light of the World 35

His Love Continues Forever 40

In Christ Alone

Eternal Hope: My Hope is Found 49

Hide Me Away 51

Be Still and Know 54

Everlasting Source 57

Abundant Provider 59

Unbroken Wonder 64

Fiery Furnace 71

Best Friend 74

True Life

The Living Dead 85

Leg Wrestling 89

Car Crash 91

Baby in the Snow 97

Chemistry Teacher 103

Chosen 109

Perpetual Beauty 112

Live in the Light 122

Singing in the Car 125

Break My Heart

Purpose of Pain 133

Purpose of Fear 138

Purpose of Our Past 142

Purpose of Hope 144

Purpose of Struggling 146

Purpose of the Bible 148

Purpose of Life: What Love Looks Like 153

Can He Still Feel the Nails?

The Way We Live 167

Immutable Determination 170

Persistent Obedience 174

Continual Mercy: A Meditation of Psalm 136 176

Paper Bag Speech 179

Rise, Let Us Go from Here

The Father's House 189

Overseer of Our Souls...194

The Sun Goes Down 196

Unwavering Focus.. 202

Take Up Your Weapons: The Armor of God................................... 206

True Bravery 209

Gateway of Hope 215

Remember: Turning on the Light... 227

Epilogue: We've Still Got It... 235

Acknowledgments 239

Part One:

The Light that Never Fades

Blue Skies and Rainbows

by Gary Mabry

Blue skies and rainbows
And sun beams from heaven
Are what I can see when
My Lord is living in me.
I know that Jesus is well and alive today.
He makes His home in my heart.
Never more will I be all alone since He
Promised me that we never would part.

Unbreakable Joy

Life is full of uncertainty and darkness. What we need most of all is light. And not just any light. We need a light that never dims, never fades. We need a light that, in fact, burns brighter in the face of opposition, trial, sin. There is only one everlasting light: God. God, the One who is merciful, faithful, and kind. God, our Savior, our glory. God, who loves us unconditionally.

"No longer will violence be heard in your land, nor ruin or destruction within your borders, but you will call your walls Salvation and your gates Praise. The sun will no more be your light by day, nor will the brightness of the moon shine on you, for the LORD will be your everlasting light, and your God will be your glory. Your sun will never set again, and your moon will wane no more; the LORD will be your everlasting light, and your days of sorrow will end. Then will all your people be righteous, and they will possess the land forever. They are the shoot I have planted, the work of my hands, for the display of my splendor. The least of you will become a thousand, the smallest a mighty nation. I am the LORD; in its time I will do this swiftly." (Isaiah 60:19-22 NKJV)

Maybe the light in your life comes from sports or social media or food. Maybe it comes from drugs, alcohol, or sex. But these things that bring temporary happiness do not fill us with unbreakable joy. Despite what Satan deceives us into believing, our joy does not come from empty escapes or even things that *can* be good but are also things we shouldn't place above God.

When I was a child, my parents got divorced. And for as long as I can remember, books were my escape. I depended on reading to comfort me, distract me, and guide me. I would spend hours and hours reading, drowning out the sounds of fighting from the kitchen or the screech of the TV from the living room. But one day, I finally realized this alone could never satisfy me or bring me everlasting joy. It was only a temporary escape, and when I closed the pages, my problems still lay unsolved like an open book before me. One day, I finally realized what God had been trying to teach me all along. I began to pray consistently, pouring out my heart to Him, confronting my problems instead of running away from them. I have never regretted choosing to pray over reading or participating in anything else. When prayer and spending time in God's Word became my coping mechanism, my joy began to grow. When I put away other distractions from my life, I could feel God's presence so much more clearly.

From the day I learned how I have loved writing. When I was young, I would regale the epic stories of knights and mermaids and dragons; I would write myself into my favorite fairy tales. On good days I would twirl around my room, imagining myself with Rapunzel's golden locks, Ariel's tail, or Belle's talking candlestick, scribbling about my adventures on any piece of paper I could find. When I was in a particularly sour mood, I pretended to be the evil Jafar, Maleficent, or Big Bad Wolf. On the in-between days I was Dopey or Mushu or Olaf, simply relaxing as the sidekick of my favorite heroes and heroines. I would write stories about anything and everything. I would write songs, poems, and movies. I would write about what was going on in my life. I would write about God. I would write about my parents. I would write about how I felt.

I can clearly remember the first writing competition I entered. I was in first grade, and the prompt was to write a poem about whatever you so desired. Having recently lost my first tooth, I decided to write about the whimsical and ever-mysterious tooth fairy.

I ended up winning third place. From then on, my writing only improved, and I kept winning writing competitions. Well, until middle school.

In seventh grade, I got really sick, and I was not myself for a long time after. For a while, I lost my sense of imagination and wonder. The world was gray, and I stopped writing with my heart. I felt empty. I couldn't find any joy.

In eighth grade, I entered a writing competition about spreading awareness for child abuse. I tried really hard, but my heart wasn't in it. I was so blinded by everything going on in my life that I couldn't even write to my full potential. My teacher told me it was good. Just good.

I did not win.

I was crushed, not because I lost, but because I knew I hadn't written with my heart. It was dry, cold, and empty, exactly how I felt at that time. I was so discouraged. I tried to find light in reading and writing, sports and school, to no avail. My world became darker.

However, God displayed His everlasting light through inspiring messages, midnight stars, and hushed hikes through a darkening forest. I regained the childlike wonder with God's creation I had missed for so long. I learned how to be joyful in all circumstances and how to view my past trials as something to be thankful for because they helped make me who I am now. I learned how to laugh again, feel again, *write* again.

This led to the spring of my freshman year, which was one of the most joyful seasons I have ever experienced in my life. I had finally gathered up the courage to enter writing competitions again. This time I wrote with all the love, light, and joy *God* had placed in my life, all the pain and heartbreak. The pieces I entered in those contests are some of the most honest things I've ever written. I wrote with my heart. I wrote with everything I had, holding back nothing. I wrote what God was calling me to.

When my teachers proofread my work, they were moved and awed by what I had written. They told me my writing was amazing. They told me it made them *feel* something: everything I had been working towards. My words weren't dry or empty or cold anymore—they were overflowing with truth and warmth and joy, so much joy. I could feel God smiling.

As I waited in anticipation for the results, I came to be at peace with both winning and losing. I trusted in God's plan. I was proud of what I had written for the first time in a while, and the light in my life finally came from God, where it should have been all along, and that was enough for me.

Over the next month, not only did I rank in three writing competitions, but I received first place. My joy was indescribable. Again, I felt God smiling. My grin mirrored His own as tears fell from my eyes. I had never experienced elation like this. When we trust in Him, He will provide abundantly. When we follow Him, His light will fill us up to the brim and overflow into the lives of others.

I did not fail to notice that when I decided to write what God placed on my heart rather than what I thought would win or what I thought others wanted to hear, I began to be successful. I was no longer consumed with people-pleasing and perfection and things that were not of God. I was consumed by God's love and will for my life and how I could shine His light through my words and actions.

I thanked God for my dry season of writing in middle school because it made my joy so much stronger when I finally broke through.

Isaiah 60 tells us that when we choose to follow God, our joy will become unbreakable because God will provide. His promises are forever, and His light is everlasting.

If we don't experience sorrow, joy won't seem as sweet. Learn to be thankful for trials because that's where we find our unbreakable joy. That's where the light that never fades emerges.

The Father of Lights

E ver since I was young, I've always loved to read. I would tear through picture book after picture book, and later, chapter after chapter of big, beautiful, old-smelling copies of classics and newly published stories and collector's editions. As I grew older, I felt a powerful calling inside my heart to do something more; it grew stronger every day. I was *made* to answer this tap on my heart. I couldn't ignore it or put it off any longer—it was time.

And so, I closed my eyes, took a deep breath, and listened. A wisp of a smile spread across my face as I finally understood Who was speaking to me and what He wanted me to do.

Do you know what happened when I began to listen to God's powerful whisper? I realized I was called to write. In a way, God prepared me to write by all the reading I had done. However, reading was no longer enough for me. I longed to share all I had learned and seen and experienced. I craved writing the same way I crave air: constantly and as an undeniable necessity.

He placed this desire to serve Him with carefully crafted words in my heart. I loved and accepted and chose to use this gift as a way to bring Him glory.

God has planted us here, the work of His hands, for His glory. The way we choose to praise Him is up to us. Whether it be through writing or singing, gardening or inventing, parenting or cooking, God has given each person He lovingly created (that's everybody) a gift. These gifts don't come from ourselves but from the Lord. It's not about our own talents or achievements: He has bestowed these gifts upon us so we can bring glory to Him.

In 1 Peter 4:8-11 (ESV), we are reminded, "Above all, keep loving one another earnestly, since love covers a multitude of sins. Show hospitality to one another without grumbling. As each has received a gift, use it to serve one another, as good stewards of God's varied grace: whoever speaks, as one who speaks oracles of God; whoever serves, as one who serves by the strength that God supplies—in order that in everything God may be glorified through Jesus Christ. To him belong glory and dominion forever and ever. Amen."

I've seen many people with unique gifts, but my mom's hospitality is one of my favorites. Proverbs 31:20 (NLT) says, "She extends a helping hand to the poor and opens her arms to the needy." No matter who she invites into our home, anyone who steps in the door is immediately put at ease by her kindness and comfort. She puts forth an effort to make others feel special and welcome. She is so intentional about making others feel at home and accepted and open. I have no doubt this is a gift from God.

James tells us that every good and perfect gift comes from the Father of lights. Our Father called us out of darkness and into His marvelous light so that we could use our talents and skills to help others find His everlasting joy. That is why Paul warns us to be persistent in using our gifts.

"Do not neglect the gift you have, which was given to you by prophecy when the council of elders laid their hands on you. Practice these things, immerse yourself in them, so that all may see your progress. Keep a close watch on yourself and on the teaching. Persist in this, for by so doing you will save both yourself and your hearers." (1 Timothy 4:14-16 ESV)

We cannot neglect the gifts God has placed in our hearts. For me, finding the time to write can be difficult amidst a busy schedule. In fact, I've been writing this book in the still moments between long trials and everyday challenges. Life has been very overwhelming lately, but I believe God is speaking to me, reminding me that in Him there is peace and sometimes what we need most is to just slow down and listen. A wise person named Rick Riordan once said, "True success requires sacrifice." And if we want to be successful in sharing the Good News, we have to cultivate our gifts so they can flourish. We have to pour hard work and consistent effort, even when we feel like we don't have the time or energy, into our gifts and into spending time with God, so that we can save both ourselves and those who are looking to us to hear the message we are called to share.

The gifts God has given us aren't meant to end with us. They were made to spread far and wide, all throughout our communities, our countries, and our world. You don't have to display your gift in a marvelous array of skill and finesse for it to be effective. Maybe your gift is the ability to listen to and comfort others. By being there for them, God might give you the opportunity to tell them about Jesus.

Maybe your gift is helping others realize what their gift is. God might provide a chance to inspire someone into action.

But there is one thing everyone must do before they can make an impact: *you must choose.* Choose to listen to God and use your gift (or gifts) how He has commanded you to wield them. Choose to sacrifice time and energy to cultivate your gift. Choose to be satisfied by doing your best with the gifts God has given you, not by seeking to be better than everyone else.

Everyone has a gift unique to them. God gave you your gift for a reason. Do not turn your back on it in pursuit of something God does not have planned. This will never turn out the way you want. Trust in Him, and He will provide an answer.

Fireflies

I wonder if fireflies flitting about in the daytime can't sleep. I wonder if they're sick with worry, silent with fear, blinded by rage. This I don't know. But I do know that when the sun sets and the sky grows dark, the fireflies shine. Sometimes it's only when darkness comes that we can shine the brightest, communicating through our stories and lights the way fireflies do.

Dear friends,

The lightning bugs appeared at the same time the sky caught fire. As I rode my bike around my neighborhood, admiring God's creation and delighting in the cool breeze, the moon beamed (though it didn't bring me dreams of Annabel Lee (that's one of my favorite poems)). I could just see the stars hidden beneath the glow of day. As I watched, they slowly began to shine brighter until it seemed as if all the dreams in the world were in reach. Somebody once said that the longer you stare at the sky, the more stars appear. I believe this to be true in more ways than the obvious, visual sense. In the same fashion, the more we open up and become willing for God to work in our lives and hearts, the more opportunities we seize, the more dreams we grasp, the more souls find Jesus. This quarantine has been a season of many challenges, and because of this, a season of much joy. I have found what James wrote to be true as well: "Count it all joy my brothers, when you face trials of various kinds, for you know that the testing of our faith produces steadfastness. And let steadfastness have its full effect, that you may be perfect and complete, lacking in nothing." (James 1:2-4 ESV)

Truly, I can't remember being more joyful than in this time of trials. I believe this is because I have found peace in God; He is made perfect in my weakness. I am thankful for suffering and joy and everything in between because it helps me strengthen my relationship with my Father in heaven.

He has answered so many prayers. And although it doesn't always turn out the way I thought or hoped it would, God's plan is perfect, and I trust in His guidance. God is my light, and I live every moment to reflect that light to others.

There is so much for me to learn and experience and overcome. I can't wait to find God in whatever blessings and hardships life throws at me. With God in my constant thoughts and steadfast heart, I lack nothing: He is all I need.

I'm praying for you to strengthen your relationship with God during this time and to shine God's light on all those you come in contact with. I am beyond thankful for all you do. You have inspired and taught and encouraged me in more ways than I can count—as numerous as the stars or the flashes of fireflies on a hot summer night. I love you wonderfully, beautifully Spirit-filled human beings. God is good. God is love. God is everything. He is my everything.

All glory be to God, Lily K. Lewis

P. S. I have some great news…

I'M COMING TO ALL FOUR WEEKS OF CAMP!

I can't wait to see old friends and make new ones, grow spiritually with others, play gaga ball and 9-square, eat mess hall food, and most of all, offer all I have in praise during lights-out singing. I love and miss you dearly. Stay bright, friends.

Just after I sent this letter, I found out that camp was canceled. Rather than letting pain destroy our faith, we have to use it to allow our faith to grow. This is the next letter I sent:

Dear Camp Family,

I cannot begin to describe the ache in my heart over camp being canceled. For the memories I won't get to make. For the mosquito bites I won't get to scratch. For the lessons I won't get to learn… Camp is truly the highlight of my year. It is a place where I feel at home with my camp family, surrounded by God's love and glory. I feel alone without lights-out singing to encourage me, speakers to inspire me, friends to confide in. I feel angry that, out of the few years I get to participate in camp as a camper, one is simply gone. And I can't get this year back.

But even if I can't get this time back, I can make the most of it. Ephesians 5:13-20 (NKJV) says, "But when anything is exposed by the light, it becomes visible, for anything that becomes visible is light. Therefore, it says, 'Awake, O sleeper, and arise from the dead, and Christ will shine on you.' Look carefully then how you walk, not as unwise but as wise, making the best use of the time, because the days are evil. Therefore, do not be foolish, but understand what the will of the Lord is… be filled with the Spirit, addressing one another in psalms and hymns and spiritual songs, singing and making melody to the Lord with your heart, giving thanks always and for everything to God the Father in the name of our Lord Jesus Christ…"

God answers prayers. Sometimes He answers them in ways that only I would understand, things nobody else would notice. Maybe you've experienced this too. I hope you have. It's amazing how God's light shines on our darkest moments to make them our greatest opportunities. We need to be challenged in our faith so God can mold us into the people He formed us to be.

God has a plan. His plan will lead us through trials and suffering to blessings and joy. My faith will not be shaken because of this. Quarantine has been full of tribulation, and because of this, great joy. I have prayed for opportunities to strengthen my faith. I have prayed for tests and challenges so I can grow closer to God because I know that when I am weakest, He is strongest. In a way, camp being canceled has been an answered prayer.

I have learned that being on fire for Christ is not reserved for camp or church or mission trips. Being genuinely on fire for Christ comes from a willingness to serve God and to be joyful in all circumstances. How can I remain sad when the sun is shining, the grass is soft beneath my feet, and the clouds dance in shapes across the sky? How can I be disappointed when the sun rises each morning, bringing a new day full of love and light and laughter? How can I question God when the fireflies appear the same time the sun sets—each dazzling hue painted by His hand, every flicker a reminder of the wonder of His creation? How can I feel lost when I can shine God's light in ways I wouldn't have been able to without this pandemic?

In the midst of any sadness I may be feeling, if there is one thing camp taught me, it's this: God is still good. When anxiety threatens to overwhelm me, God reminds me there is nothing He cannot do. When disappointment drags me down, God whispers of the hope of our salvation. When fear seems to control me, God gives me peace. In the face of uncertainty, God is our only constant. He will not fail. He will not fall. He will not forget.

God is good, and I refuse to doubt. I will have courage and make the most of this season of struggles. I encourage you to do the same.

All glory be to God, Lily Lewis

Chasing Sunsets and Seeking the Lord

I want to spend my life chasing sunsets and seeking the Lord.

I held on for dear life to the back of a golf cart at the thrilling speed of fifteen miles per hour. It had just rained, a gentle mist, a summer shower. My friend's house sits on the shore of a lake surrounded by an enchanted forest. To me, all forests are magical, as if each time you step into the green, something extraordinary might happen. How could they not be when the Lord has designed each leaf, blade of grass, frog, and flower so fearfully, so wonderfully? Along the road, glimpses of many lakes can be seen through a shroud of dense trees, deer with white-speckled hides prancing along the outskirts, wildflowers dusting the edges, whirling by as we sang "Reckless Love" by Corey Asbury at the top of our lungs. The wind whipped my hair into a massive tangle, and a cicada flew down my shirt, causing me to screech and momentarily panic, nearly falling off the golf cart, before collapsing into a fit of laughter.

Earlier that day, and during the majority of quarantine, I felt alone, longing with all my heart for things I couldn't have, at least not at that exact moment. I missed camp so much my heart ached. I missed Nicaragua so much I couldn't breathe. I missed feeling the presence of the Lord I can't feel in the same way anywhere else. Most of all, I craved the intense joy that comes from lights-out singing, hugging every child at the school in Nicaragua, flying above the clouds in a sky so beautiful strangers become friends. I wanted to sing praise around a bonfire, voice thick with smoke, fingers sticky with s'mores. I wanted to lay under stars which always seem so much brighter at camp in a time of midnight prayer. I wanted to serve rice to teachers and students and families who are not only hungry for nourishment, but hungry for a relationship with God.

I missed the rats and bats that scuttle and scratch in the ceiling above my bed in León, Nicaragua. I missed the heat and the sun and the mosquitoes. I would have given anything to be bitten by a mosquito at camp because, well, it would mean I was at camp. I would have wept to hear the flap of wings or the pitter-patter of feet above my head because it would mean I'd be there in León, surrounded by Christians who love our wonderful Savior and opportunities to spread God's Word.

If I'm being completely honest, the showers at camp are worse than the showers in Nicaragua, and yes, both are moldy and cold and covered with bugs. They flood often, there's hair stuck in the drain, and the occasional frog might hop in, too. Someone always forgets their shampoo or hairbrush or towel, and there are thirty other girls packed into two small rooms with about ten showers and toilets. It's muggy and hot and gross. And yet, I would take joy in being in that stuffy room if it meant I could laugh and cry and learn about Jesus with my friends.

Many people missed a lot of things during the coronavirus pandemic: sports, school, eating out, going to the movies. Many people also missed loved ones and church and community. Despite this, in a way, I'm thankful for the pandemic. Through it, God taught me how to choose peace amidst chaos, deal with disappointment, and find light in the dark. It wasn't always easy. Friends got sick, protests raged across the country, all events were canceled, rescheduled, or virtual. When I found myself feeling lost, doubtful, or weary, I'd walk. I witnessed spring quietly unfurl for the first time. I watched the breath of God fill the world and make it bright once more. When I walked, I prayed. I listened to God's whisper, surrendering everything at His feet.

My favorite time to walk is sunset. The sun drowns the world in gold as it sinks toward the horizon, dragging any morsel of doubt from my heart and melting it into wonder. "Amaze me, God." I would whisper. And whether it was with rosy clouds fashioned in the shape of the frosted animal crackers I loved as a kid, startling laughter from deep within my chest, or the way the sinking sunlight warmed my freckled skin, thawing me from the outside in, God answered my prayer each day. Some days a particularly lovely rose would catch my eye, or a proud sunflower would humble me to the glory of God's creation.

"My Lord, my God! I need you. Help me!" I begged.

The rustling leaves sang a song in the breeze of a Savior who was oh so near. He heard my cries. I knew that He was there. I could feel Him in my heart on those peaceful walks, in the sound of the trees and my footsteps. I fought fear with faith. I battled anxiety with trust and joy. I destroyed doubt with awe; God guided me through every step. In the dark, He lifted my head to the stars, never letting me stray, always leading me back to Him. He dried my tears and reminded me of His glory.

As I laughed with my friends on the golf cart, I remembered my constant prayer during quarantine: "God, amaze me." I closed my eyes, wind whipping around me, and prayed. When I opened my eyes, the sun was beginning to set. Lavender faded into blush, and blush blossomed into gold. *That* smile, the quirked grin that springs up when you realize what

He's whispering, spread across my face. What I craved was intense joy, a joy that I felt only came from adventures and mission trips and dreams come true. But God was teaching me to be content. He was teaching me that the steady joy that comes from trusting Him is good and that I don't have to constantly be seeking Him in over-the-top ways to feel His presence. More often than not, it's in the quiet moments that we hear His voice the most.

1 Kings 19:11-13 (NKJV) says, "Then He said, 'Go out, and stand on the mountain before the Lord.' And behold, the Lord passed by, and a great strong wind tore into the mountains and broke the rocks in pieces before the Lord, but the Lord was not in the wind; after the wind was an earthquake but the Lord was not in the earthquake; and after the earthquake a fire, but the Lord was not in the fire; and after the fire a still small voice. So it was, when Elijah heard it, that he wrapped his face in his mantle and went and stood in the entrance of the cave. Suddenly a voice came to him, and said, 'What are you doing here Elijah?'"

I want to spend my life chasing sunsets and seeking the Lord. I feel most content when I am walking and praying. I am satisfied, like Elijah, when I recognize the Lord's voice and choose to listen to His quiet whisper. How can anyone see a sunset and not believe that God is real and good and alive? How can they not hear His voice?

When we reach out to others, show them God's love, share the humble glories of God's creation. Show them the gentle sunset, show them the delicate lily, show them calm waters and white-speckled deer prancing in meadows. Show them God's everlasting light, one small step at a time. Show them what true joy looks like in Jesus. Show them hope, and I promise God will work in their hearts and answer your prayers if you remain patient.

Treasure

As kids, we all treasure small knick-knacks we find and toys that comfort us. We adore our soft blanket, brown teddy bear, or favorite book. We cling to our relationships with our parents or friends or childhood sweethearts. We admire the beauties of nature: flowers, rocks, ladybugs. We treasure anything that captures our attention, anything that fascinates us. We allow the object of our interest to draw us in, enthrall us, ensnare us. Our thoughts become centered around our treasure; we can think or speak of nothing else. There is no room for anything else in our attention and focus.

When we grow up, what we treasure shifts to things like money and cars and jobs. Above everything else, we value promotions and houses and contests. Our lives are no longer about recognizing our blessings and sharing them with others—our purpose becomes discovering how we can gain more and give less. It becomes about being the best.

Have you ever had a small child come up to you and share about the thing that fascinates them? They treat it as if it were a precious jewel, eyes wide with amazement and joy as they show it to you. Are we as excited to share our wonder with God as children are their precious treasures?

In Matthew 6:19-21 (NIV), it says, "Do not store up for yourselves treasure on earth, where moth and vermin destroy and where thieves break in and steal. But store up for yourselves treasures in heaven, where moth and vermin do not destroy and where thieves do not break in and steal. For where your treasure is, there your heart will be also."

Are you storing up godly treasure or worldly treasure? Do you cherish your blessings, allowing gratitude for God's goodness to encourage you, or do you treasure your possessions, placing them above your Savior?

One of the greatest gifts God has given us is His Word. Without it, we would be lost in times of darkness, without hope and without assurance of God's promises and purpose for our lives. Romans 15:4 (ESV) says, "For whatever was written in former days was written for our instruction, that through endurance and through the encouragement of the Scriptures we might have hope."

Many Christians, in the past and present day, do not have access to the Bible. They rely on missionaries to tell them the Good News. In several countries, owning a Bible or preaching about Jesus is illegal and met with severe consequences. Some Christians pray for years before they can receive a Bible. Some are arrested, tortured, or killed simply for owning one. Others make incredibly long journeys to receive God's Word, struggling against corrupt authorities and oppression every step of the way.

In America, Bibles are easy to come by. According to various studies and surveys, approximately eight out of ten Americans have a Bible, or Bibles, in their household, regardless of whether they read it or not. Imagine how painful it must be for a Christian in a foreign country to know there is an abundance of Bibles in the United States *that people are not even reading*. Imagine how much it hurts God. So many people own a copy of His Word, which is His gift to us, and have never even opened it.

Do you treasure the Bible enough that you would travel hundreds of miles to find one, pray for years in continual hope and confidence to receive one, risk being arrested, killed, or tortured for owning one? How dedicated are you to following His commandments? Do you treasure His Words, which were written out of love and mercy and the hope that each one of us would choose Him? Is your heart completely focused on Scripture?

If we do not treasure God's Word, our heart is not entirely with God. Scripture tells us that we shouldn't put outer beauty or bodily strength on a pedestal because these things will fade. Instead, it tells us to cultivate inner purity and faithfulness, hope and love, mercy and wisdom, in our lives. These things will last forever.

To live a life of everlasting light, we have to treasure God's Word, promises, wisdom, and blessings. If we don't treasure these things, we not only lose our wonder with God's glory, but we lose our ability to hope and fulfill God's purpose.

So how can we shift our treasure from worldly things to holy things? We have to recognize God's purpose for our lives, choose to hope, and ask for wisdom. We have to realize how precious God's Word is.

Understanding God's will for us helps us keep our eyes focused on godly treasure. In Matthew 28:19-20 (ESV), Jesus shares this command with His disciples: "'Go therefore and make disciples of all nations, baptizing them in the name of the Father and of the Son and of the Holy Spirit, teaching them to observe all that I have commanded you. And behold, I am with you always, to the very end of this age.'"

Our purpose as followers of Jesus is to tell others about the Savior and what He sacrificed for us. It may be uncomfortable at times, awkward, or even frightening, but it will always be worth it. In 1 John, the writer also tells us that our purpose is to love others as God loves us, unconditionally and without restraint. If you genuinely love others, wouldn't you want them to hear about Jesus so they could be saved? A huge part of valuing godly treasure is learning to hold our purpose and love for others sacredly in our hearts, remembering them as a gift from the Father.

Once we recognize our purpose and choose to abide by it, we must choose to hope. Hope is one of the greatest gifts God has blessed us with. Over and over again in Scripture, hope is mentioned as a blessing, a promise, and, most importantly, a choice. Hope isn't something that comes naturally. It's something we have to decide to live by each morning. It's something we have to discover for ourselves in God's Word. We can't treasure God's Word without being certain that it's true or without hoping for a better eternal life to come.

That is why we follow God's commandments. For the sacrifice Jesus made for us, for the God who created us, and for the hope He has given us, a treasure that can never be lost, taken, or destroyed.

Jeremiah 29:11-13 (ESV) says, "For I know the plans I have for you, declares the Lord, plans for welfare and not for evil, to give you a hope and a future. Then you will call upon me and come and pray to me, and I will hear you. You will seek me and find me when you seek me with all your heart."

What is the best gift you've ever received? Maybe it's a toy you got for Christmas as a child or a letter from a loved one. Maybe it's a wedding ring or a long-awaited child. Maybe it was a bouquet of flowers on a rainy day or a trip to your favorite place in the world. Whatever it may be, that gift is something you probably treasure very much, something you hold close to your heart, something that makes you smile when you feel discouraged.

Whatever the best gift you've received in a physical sense may be, the gift of hope and purpose God has given us is infinitely more significant. Physical treasure is ephemeral. It won't come with you from this life to the next. But heavenly treasure is eternal, everlasting, and unending. It will remain with you forever.

But to receive this heavenly treasure, live God's purpose for our lives, and choose hope, we must ask God for wisdom to determine what holy treasure our hearts should focus on.

Satan will try to make you believe that worldly treasure is better than godly treasure. He will try to convince you that immediate gratification trumps eternal contentment. He will attempt to trick you into trading hope for fear, purpose for sin, and wisdom for foolishness. He will try to make you doubt. He will endeavor to shake your heart's focus on God and His Word with lies and schemes and temptations. If we don't ask God for wisdom, Satan will easily defeat us.

James 1:5-6 (ESV) says this, "If any of you lacks wisdom, let him ask God, who gives generously to all without reproach, and it will be given to him. But let him ask in faith, with no doubting, for the one who doubts is like a wave of the sea that is driven and tossed by the wind."

Are you confident that God will answer your prayers? Has the doubt Satan attempts to instill within you already struck your heart? There is no situation from which God cannot untangle you, even if it has. Reach out to Him in prayer and He will help you. Reach out to Him in trust, and He will guide you. Reach out to Him in humble confidence, and He will give you wisdom.

Focusing on heavenly treasure is not about severing all ties to earth— it's about knowing what's most important and choosing to focus on the thing that will bring you true joy through Christ.

God's Word is beautiful and uplifting and awe-inspiring. It is filled with songs and stories and praise. It is overflowing with forgiveness and peace and love. It is precious. It is holy. It is sacred. It tells of victory and blessings and fulfilled promises and prophecies. It sings of everything that is good, pushes away whatever is evil. There is no hate, no fear, because Jesus's light has overcome the darkness. In the face of trials and pain and grief, God's Word provides endurance and encouragement and hope.

To live a life of everlasting light, we have to choose to find hope, purpose, and wisdom in God's Word, one of our most treasured gifts, and hold it at the center of our hearts and our lives.

The Message That Continues Forever

1 Peter 1:23-25 (NCV) says, "You have been born again, and this new life did not come from something that dies, but from something that cannot die. You were born again through God's living message that continues forever. The Scripture says, 'All people are like the grass, and all their glory is like the flowers of the field. The grass dies and the flowers fall, but the word of the Lord will live forever.' And this is the word that was preached to you."

The Gospel is immortal. It never dies out or fades away. It is always applicable. It is always true. It is always relatable. The Bible was designed so every story could connect with anyone from any time, place, or walk of life.

One of the reasons this Gospel message continues forever is because it will always be relevant. Think about all the classic books of literature you study and read in school. They are "timeless" classics because their message was true in the past, is true in the present, and will still be true in the future. They are classics because people will always relate to some aspect of the book: theme, setting, characters, struggles, triumphs, pain, love.

And the Bible contains the greatest struggle and triumph of all—the most extraordinary love story ever written. The Bible describes the story of Jesus.

Jesus was sent to earth to die for our sins so that we might have eternal life. But for Him to be sacrificed, He had to live a perfect life free from sin, a life we could never live, a feat we could never even dream to accomplish.

Jesus can relate to us, to everyone. Although He never sinned, Jesus was still tempted. Did you know that? Even though Jesus lived a perfect life, there was still temptation all around Him. Living a perfect life wasn't easy for Him, but He was made perfect through the struggle, made relatable to us through His temptations. We are tempted by cell phones, peer pressure, alcohol, drugs, and so many other things surrounding us. In a similar way, Jesus suffered through grief, sorrow, and emotional pain from betrayal and knowing the agony that was to come, that had to be endured on the cross. But He still prayed for God's will to be done.

Jesus endured beatings and whips and humiliation—even mockery. Nails were driven through His hands and feet to mount Him upon the cross, the most shameful death possible during that period, and all so that we might see His goodness, repent, and change our lives for good, for *God*.

Jesus was sent to die for everyone, so His story connects with everyone. Jesus is a gift to us from God, the ultimate sacrifice. John 3:16 (NIV) strikingly states, "For God so loved the world that he gave his one and only Son, that whoever believes in him shall not perish but have eternal life." Can you imagine giving up your own child to die for a world full of sinners and liars and cheaters? Would you have done it? *Could* you have done it? Yet God loves us so much that He sent His only Son to die for us, so that we could live in harmony with Him in heaven one day. God chooses to focus on the good and not the bad. He doesn't see us as sinners. He sees us as beautiful, lost sheep whom He longs to return home, that He might bless and protect and keep us. God wants us to find Him, and He tells us exactly how to discover His dwelling place. All He asks us to do is believe.

Jeremiah 29:13 (NIV) promises, "You will seek me and find me when you seek me with all your heart." *When we believe we will find God, we will seek Him with our whole heart. When we seek God with all our heart, we will find Him.*

The *message* of Jesus continues forever because *Jesus* continues forever. After He died on the cross, He was buried in the grave. But the story didn't end there. After He was buried for three days, He rose from the grave. He rose to show us that there is nothing He cannot conquer. Not even death can overcome the power of God.

The Gospel continues forever because we forever have the need to share it. As Christians, it should be our joy and our desire to bring others to heaven with us. Jesus relates this mission to His disciples in Matthew 28:18-20 (NIV). "Then Jesus came to them and said, 'All authority in heaven and on earth has been given to me. Therefore, go and make disciples of all nations, baptizing them in the name of the Father and of the Son and of the Holy Spirit, and teaching them to obey everything I have commanded you. And surely I am with you always, to the very end of the age.'"

The age of Jesus in the flesh may have ended, but the spiritual age of Jesus is eternal. When Jesus commanded His disciples to share the Good News everywhere they go, He wasn't just speaking to those who were present. *Jesus was speaking to every person who would ever follow Him.* He has called you to share the message that continues forever, so what are you waiting for?

Everyone has a deep desire to know Jesus, to have a relationship with Him, even if they are unaware of it until someone comes along to help them or something happens that reveals the truth. In Ecclesiastes, Solomon writes about how he tried everything under the sun to find satisfaction, joy, and purpose. The only place he found it was in God's open arms. Nothing but God can fill the hole in our hearts. The Gospel continues forever because it is the only thing that can fill our hearts.

If we choose to share the beautiful message of Jesus with joy, everlasting light will shine into our lives and the lives of those around us, even on the darkest, rainiest, dreariest days. This is a promise of God's bright smile over the good work that brings souls to His kingdom in heaven. Jesus's message continues forever because His love for us continues forever. Amen.

God Will Provide
the Words

1 Peter 3:13-18 (NLT) says, "Now, who will want to harm you if you are eager to do good? But even if you suffer for doing what is right, God will reward you for it. So, don't worry or be afraid of their threats. Instead, you must worship Christ as Lord of your life. And if someone asks about your hope as a believer, always be ready to explain it. But do this gently and respectfully. Keep your conscience clear. Then if people speak against you, they will be ashamed when they see what a good life you live because you belong to Christ. Remember, it is better to suffer for doing good, if that is what God wants, than to suffer for doing wrong! Christ suffered for our sins once and for all time. He never sinned, but he died for sinners to bring you safely home to God. He suffered physical death, but he was raised to life in the Spirit."

Scripture is God-breathed. The writers of the Bible were filled with the Holy Spirit. God gave them the exact words He wanted people to read and live by forever. God gave Paul the words and Moses the words. He gave David, Solomon, Peter, and Luke the words. The Lord also gave Nehemiah, Matthew, James, Jude, and John the words. He gave everyone who ever defended His precious, holy Name the words and the courage to overcome the lies Satan makes people believe.

In the same way, God still gives us the words. He provides the words when we don't know how to comfort a friend. He provides the words when we are called to defend our faith. He provides the words to inspire people when we are too afraid to speak in front of an audience. God provides the words.

The encouraging messages I send out each week are not my words, but God's. This very book is God speaking through me. I am the pen and God is the writer. He is my source of creativity. The Lord provided a way to be a light through my gift of writing, a way to encourage others through uplifting messages and books and even handwritten letters.

During quarantine, I couldn't see my friends and loved ones in person, so I decided to write letters to them. I had so much fun writing these letters and sending them to people. But it wasn't just about having fun, and it wasn't just something to do when I was bored. It was about showing others the hope I had in God's plan so they could learn to hope too. I wrote letters to encourage others, cheer them up, and make them laugh when they needed to release some stress. I wrote to share with them the message of God. In these letters, God provided the words. Somehow, God always gives me the words that someone needed to hear that day. That can only come from the Lord when we choose to dedicate our lives to Him.

Don't be afraid to share the Good News because you don't have a speech prepared. Don't worry about what you will say when questioned about your faith: God will provide the words for you the same way He has provided for the authors of the Bible and for Christians in all types of situations throughout history.

Luke 21:14-15 (NIV) says, "But make up your mind not to worry beforehand how you will defend yourselves. For I will give you words and wisdom that none of your adversaries will be able to resist or contradict."

God will provide the words. All you have to do is let go and choose to trust Him, allowing Him to speak His gentle message of everlasting light through *you*.

Perspective

Some people say that when they look at the stars, it makes them feel small and insignificant compared to the vast expanse of the sky and all its mysteries. It confounds them. It awes them. It sometimes even haunts them, the loneliness of the infinite stretch of blackness and planets and lifelessness. It frightens them.

The opposite is true for me. When I look at the stars, I feel like the whole universe is at my fingertips, my dreams in reach if only I dare to try. I feel so full of hope and wonder and gratitude that I might burst. I feel alive, amazed, connected. When I look at the stars everything becomes clearer. For me, inspiration, joy, and determination can all stem from the silvery pinpricks of light in the night sky.

It's as if everything clicks into place when I look at the stars. I can feel God wrap His arms around me, an embrace of light in the darkness. I can see God's will for me, written in the constellations He so lovingly weaved into the night.

Psalm 8:3-4 (ESV) says, "When I look at your heavens, the work of your fingers, the moon and the stars, which you have set in place, what is man that you are mindful of him, and the son of man that you care for him?"

It's a blessing that God created something so wonderful. He set each and every star in the sky. Every planet, ring, asteroid, and moon, God created. He placed everything perfectly, like the sun and earth, so we could live. God made all these things for us to hope, ponder, and dream about. God made the sky and stars so we could find Him and bring glory to Him through our joy and dreams and wonder.

Colossians 1:16-17 (NIV) tells us, "For in him all things were created: things in heaven and on earth, visible and invisible, whether thrones or powers or rulers or authorities; all things have been created through him and for him. He is before all things, and in him all things hold together."

God is alive. He has always been alive and will live forever. He came before everything, and when He decided to craft this world from nothing but His words, He intended to use it for His purpose. His purpose is for us to praise Him and love Him and share Him. His purpose for us is to be amazed and humbled by the world He spoke into existence. His purpose for us is to laugh and hope and dream. His purpose is for us to *live*, for there is nothing greater than the gift of life.

Psalm 136:1-9 (NIV) says this, "Give thanks to the Lord, for He is good. His love endures forever. Give thanks to the God of gods. His love endures forever. Give thanks to the Lord of lords: His love endures forever. To Him who alone does great wonders, His love endures forever. Who by His understanding made the heavens, His love endures forever. Who spread out the earth upon the waters, His love endures forever. Who made the great lights—His love endures forever. The sun to govern the day, His love endures forever. The moon and stars to govern the night, His love endures forever."

God made all these things—wonders and stars and moons—because His love endures forever. God created everything for a purpose out of love. He loves us unconditionally, irrevocably, and eternally. That's why He gives us our ultimate objective: a godly conviction to love.

I can't even begin to imagine what God's voice must sound like. I can't fathom the love that would emanate from every word He spoke. What would it be like to hear the voice of the One who spoke everything into existence? To hear the All-Powerful Savior calling to you? To hear the love and joy and hope in His song?

Although I cannot picture His literal voice, I can feel His whisper in my heart. His voice is soft as rain yet hard as thunder. Kind as a father yet teaching discipline and commanding respect. High as the tallest tree yet deep as the bottom of the sea. God consists of all things and He created all things. Everything He created, He created with a small part of Himself.

When we look at the stars, we should see the everlasting light of God shining bright before our eyes. He made the stars so we could see His goodness and praise Him. He formed the stars so we could form a relationship with Him. All we have to do to hear God's voice is take a moment, a still and quiet moment, to watch the stars and wonder. God will speak to you through His creation, just as He intended. You just have to choose to be still and know.

In everything, God provides abundantly. The stars are no exception. There are innumerable lights in the sky, each a promise to us of God's presence, a gift of peace and wonder, and the assurance of a hope and a future. I am beyond thankful God created all the marvels of this world; He fashioned the stars, moons, and skies with us in mind. To give us hopes and dreams and determination.

When I look at the stars, I think of all the things God has taught me and all the things He's teaching me right now. I think of His promise that Abraham would be blessed with countless children, as many as the stars in the sky. I think of hope in the darkness. I think of everlasting light. I think of true life, life spent wondering at God's creation and chasing Him wherever I may walk.

Every night I peek out my window to see if the stars are out, no matter where I happen to be. When they shine bright, I smile and thank God. When the night is cloudy or rain falls to the earth, I smile and thank God. Even when I can't see the stars, I know they are there. In the same way, God will never leave us, not even when life is dark and messy.

Hebrews 11:1-3 (NIV) says these words, "Now faith is confidence in what we hope for and assurance about what we do not see. This is what the ancients were commended for. By faith we understand that the universe was formed at God's command, so that what is seen was not made by what is visible."

It takes faith to believe that the stars are still shining, that God is still present, even when we can't see it. It's a choice we have to make. We can either choose to hope or be lost in the darkness. We can choose to have faith, or we can choose to lose confidence. We can choose to find God in His creation, or we can choose to leave His masterpiece unadmired. It's up to us to decide. It's up to *you*.

One of my favorite worship songs by Leeland, "Way Maker," says this,

"You are here working in this place
I worship You.
Even when I don't see it, You're working
Even when I don't feel it, You're working
You never stop. You never stop working
Way Maker, Miracle Worker, Promise Keeper
Light in the darkness, my God
that is who You are."

Even when we can't see it, God is working, and He will never give up on us. Don't give up on Him. He will work miracles in your life if you choose to view it through a lens of everlasting light, if you choose to open your heart to a new perspective of His creation.

We are never alone or unimportant; we shouldn't be afraid. God will clear the way for you to follow Him. He will speak to you through His creation.

He will keep all His promises. He will answer your prayers. He will flip the switch of our darkest times by filling us with the light of hope, the light that never fades.

Light of the World

God's light shines bright. Nothing will ever change that. Not darkness, not fear, not sadness. Nothing. God's light will shine on every aspect of our lives if we open our hearts to Him.

Psalm 36:9 (NKJV) says, "For with You is the fountain of life; In Your light we see light."

I interpret this verse to mean that in God's light, His mercy, love, and forgiveness, we can find our light, the thing that makes our lives overflow with joyful abundance. In God's light we can discover our passions, see the bright side of any situation, and grow to know our Savior more intimately. If you need to feel God's light and see your life through a newer, brighter perspective, open your heart to God—He will provide.

But in order to open our hearts to God, we have to ask ourselves a question: what is the light of the world?

This is a question I considered for a long time before the answer came to me. Of course, the most obvious answer is Jesus. But as I thought about it more deeply, I realized it was something even more than that. There is one thing that made Jesus stand out above all else: love. Love is the light of the world. Passion is what inspires the world. Emotion is what brings everything to life. It's what sets apart the most distinguished painters, writers, and musicians; the true mark of success as an artist is the ability to make someone feel something. It is love. All of it is love.

As I was writing this book, I was slowly falling in love. At first, I was scared to share anything about my love life because I was afraid of what people would say, and I was worried that we might break up and then it would just be awkward. But then one of the most beautiful moments of my life happened, and I realized that to write this book about how I've experienced God's everlasting light without mentioning one of the main lights in my life would be dishonest. There are many different stages of life, and I'm happy to share my experiences of all aspects of my teenage years. God likes to work in interesting ways sometimes, and this may be what someone needed to get through something. So, here goes nothing. This is my memory of the day that I finally discovered the light of the world. And I am not afraid to share it with you:

The first time I met Seth Pratt was on a field trip in seventh grade. The funny thing is a guy I liked at the time was the one to introduce me to him. We hit it off immediately and became close friends over the next two years. We had lots of inside jokes and often confided in each other, even asking for dating advice.

During the summer of quarantine we didn't talk very much. When I sent out letters to my friends and family, I considered sending one to him, but I was too scared. I didn't want him to think I had a crush on him and ruin our friendship. At the time, I had no idea he would become my first love.

Towards the end of the summer, we started texting about what classes we had that year and which classes we had together. I saw him for the first time after six months of quarantine at open house. I didn't even recognize him at first. Over the break, he had grown several inches taller, his shoulders had gotten broader, and his hair had become curlier. Six months ago, he was so cute and dorky. But now, he was just plain cute.

My heart started beating faster, and suddenly I was nervous to be around him.

At soccer practice, I mentioned him to some of my friends, and one of them agreed he was cute. For some reason, I felt a little jealous and territorial. And that's when it clicked: I had a crush on my guy best friend. I liked Seth Pratt, and I didn't think he liked me back.

On the first day of school, he parked beside me, and we walked in together. And then the next day and the next day and the next. We would talk and laugh and joke with one another in the morning, and it never failed to brighten my day.

My best friend, Hannah, knew I liked him before I would even admit it. Again, I was afraid to ruin our friendship, and I didn't want to make things awkward. Things continued like this until one day, he asked me for advice about two girls he liked. He said that one of them he was kind of interested in, and the other he really liked, but he wasn't sure if she liked him back. Our mutual friend Draegan is the one who convinced me to be honest with him about how I felt; I cannot thank him enough for pushing me to make a phone call that changed my life.

We talked and it turned out that he had liked me since freshman year. I had been oblivious the whole time. We hung out for a few weeks and went on a couple of dates, and after some long talks about what we wanted out of a relationship, we decided to make it official.

Six months later, we were still going strong. Although we would occasionally have small fights or disagreements, we always talked and forgave one another by the end of the day.

One afternoon, however, we had a fight and we were both pretty rude to each other. We were both so stressed with finals that we said some things we didn't really mean.

Later that day, a few friends and I went to a new cookie shop, and I decided to bring him a few cookies. I firmly believe that chocolate is one of the best ways to ask for forgiveness. When I arrived at his house, the sun was gently fading from day to night, the stars taking up their positions in the sky slowly, one by one. I crawled on top of my car with my keys, my phone, and the cookies. When he opened the garage door, I started playing one of my favorite songs to jokingly sing to him: "I Love You Baby" by Frank Sinatra.

He walked over with a big smile to match my own and hopped on top of the car to sit with me. The music faded as I asked him for forgiveness and held up a cookie I picked out for him. He laughed as he took a bite, and just like that he forgave me; I forgave him, too.

We sat and shared the cookies and talked things through. Out of nowhere, he said, "I love you, Lily."

I blushed, tucking my hair behind my ear and looking to the side. "I love you too, Seth."

It was not the first time we had said "I love you," but this time felt different. He looked me in the eyes and told me everything he loved about me. All of it was so, so sweet, but there was one thing he said that stuck with me.

"Lily, one of the reasons I love you is because you have brought me closer to God. During quarantine, I started to fall away from God. I was so out of touch with my emotions. But then you came along. You've helped me grow so much as a person and in my spiritual life. Thank you. All I can say is thank you."

Tears glistened in my eyes when I responded. "For so long I refused to accept any emotion at all. I was afraid to feel. But then one moment at camp, a prayer under a midnight sky, changed my life. Ever since, I have always chosen to feel no matter what, not in spite of my fear, but because I know God will draw me nearer to Him through it. Refusing to feel is worse than feeling the bad things like anger, jealousy, or sorrow. Because without the bad things, we could never truly experience just how wonderful the good things are."

The next part was even harder to admit. I whispered, "Sometimes, I'm still a little afraid to feel deeply because it opens the door to heartbreak and pain. I panic and try to push people away. I'm sorry."

He gently angled my chin until I was looking him in the eye again. "Lily, I won't let you push me away. I'm not going anywhere, girl."

I smiled as he gave me a big hug and then said something that means more to me than anyone could possibly understand. "Lily, you are my moment at camp."

Right then, fireflies appeared to glow in the dark spaces between the stars, illuminating the fields of grass right before the sun dipped below the horizon completely.

"You changed my life for the better. You have helped me to find God again. You have helped me to heal and to love and to feel. I love you."

We sat on top of my car in his driveway, the music a welcome presence in the lyrics of our love for one another, and talked for a while. Just talked. Before I had to leave, I closed my eyes, his arms embracing me, his chin resting atop my head, and thanked God for this boy who helped to show me the light of the world—a pure and true love that only grows stronger with challenges. It was a night I will never forget.

So what, if I'm a sixteen-year-old girl? I love God and I love Seth and I love everyone else, too. That is the light of my life. I hope that this light will shine in your life, too. All you have to do is choose and wait for God to get to work. Don't be afraid to feel. Be honest with yourself and others. Take a chance. You might have already met the love of your life, and you just don't know it yet.

Open your eyes and see, dear friend. The Light of the World shines brightly for all to see. Open your eyes and dream. The Light of the World is alive, and in this light we can find the hope, passion, and purpose that will give glow to our lives, for all to see and praise God.

His Love Continues Forever

As humans, our love is often conditional. We only go so far out of our way to do nice things for those we care about. We don't want to be inconvenienced. We don't want to be interrupted. Often, we just want people to leave us alone.

When others ask us to do something, we shouldn't have to plaster a smile on our faces and act like we're happy to do it—all for show. When we choose to do something kind it shouldn't feel obligated or forced. It should flow naturally, genuinely, and without complaint from our hearts. This is something I need to work on, too.

How often have you recognized the right thing to do but didn't do it because it was too difficult? How many times have you thought of something nice to do but turned your back because it required too much time, effort, or money? How often have you heard God's whisper but failed to respond? How many times have we been given the opportunity to love like Jesus and chosen not to?

"So, whoever knows the right thing to do and fails to do it," James 4:7 (ESV) tells us, "for him it is sin."

This verse doesn't say it is sin for him *only if* the right thing to do is too hard. It doesn't say it is sin for him *only if* you don't have the time or money. It doesn't say it is sin for him *only if* you don't have the energy. James 4:17 (ESV) says, "So, whoever knows the right thing to do and fails to do it, for him it is sin."

It's straightforward: choosing not to do the right thing is a sin no matter what challenges lay in the way. Don't make excuses. Choose to love as you are called to.

The amazing thing about the love of Jesus is that it's all about interruptions and inconveniences and patience. No matter what Jesus was busy doing, He *always* shared the Good News. He stopped to heal, preach, and work miracles whenever people needed Him. He knew His mission of coming to earth to save us from our sins wouldn't be about Him being comfortable and pampered and well-rested. It was about Him living selflessly, at all times, to set a perfect example for us to follow today.

Jesus's love takes action. 1 John 3:18 (NIV) says this, "Dear children, let us not love with words or speech but with actions and in truth."

No matter what, Jesus always stopped to help others, listen to those who were hurting, and share the Good News with people who were searching for more. The reason He chose to do this? He loves others unconditionally. He loves *us* unconditionally.

Jesus must have been tired a lot of the time. Traveling all over, teaching and performing miracles every day, defending Himself to people who didn't believe in Him or who wanted to cause Him harm with love and gentleness instead of hate. It's not easy to choose love, but Jesus chose it every time, no matter the consequences, even to the point of being sacrificed on the cross for us. He could only do this through constantly choosing to draw His love, patience, and hope from God, the eternal source of all good things. Jesus's love never ran out because God's love never runs out. Jesus must have been tired a lot of the time, but true love takes action, so He never ceased doing the right thing.

Jesus wasn't treated as the King He is. He was born in a pile of hay in the modern-day equivalent of a barn and lain to rest in a manger, a feeding basket for animals. The Savior of the world was born in the humblest of places imaginable. He was never super rich; He never wore fine clothes or ate luxurious food. He was ridiculed, laughed at, and challenged when He should have been praised. Jesus didn't come to earth to be comfortable. If He had, His love wouldn't be unconditional. If He had, we probably wouldn't look at Him the same way.

But He *did* come to reach out to us—out of His comfort zone and into our hearts. And He will never back away when things go wrong. Because true love takes action, He never gives up.

Jesus was interrupted daily by people who were sick, diseased, and hurting, inside and out. They needed someone to help them. Jesus chose to be that person, never angry or upset about inconveniences, but accepting them with a patient smile. He knew God was smiling down on Him. Jesus took joy in interruptions because love stops and takes action, regardless of what is happening around you.

Sometimes I'm *terrible* at being patient. I get antsy or tired or frustrated with people and situations. We all have those days. But on those days, like Jesus, we still have to choose to love. Even on bad days, true love takes action. We shouldn't worship God in spite of our busy schedules—we should make time for Him because of them. Jam-packed plans aren't an excuse to skip out on reading your Bible. It's a reason to set some time aside to pray and talk to Jesus about all that's going on in your life. Our lives need to be interrupted with spontaneous praise and inconvenient opportunities more often. A lot of the time, those are the moments we feel closest to God: in the situations we never expected to find Him in.

I used to hate inconveniences and interruptions, complaining and making a fuss. And then one day, when I realized I sincerely wanted to start loving like Jesus, I started praying for them. I realized the only way to grow in patience was to struggle through situations that challenged me. God *really* answers prayers, and boy, did He answer this one.

All of a sudden my life was filled with interruptions like never before. However, instead of becoming harder to love like Jesus, it became easier. There were the small, everyday interruptions like helping people with things they should know how to do, babysitting my siblings, and losing something I needed. And then there were the big interruptions like the COVID-19 pandemic, a car crash, and the death of loved ones. Inspiration for writing has a habit of striking me right before I plan on going to bed, but even this interruption I chose to say yes to even though it meant losing a couple minutes of sleep. I felt God tapping on my heart; I saw Him working every time I was tempted to lose my patience or give up. Through it all, I learned to have the patient love of Jesus.

There were many days I messed up, and many more mistakes will come in the future, but patience and love come a little more naturally now. I have learned to find joy in inconveniences, because I know they are an answered prayer from God, a way to grow closer to Him, and an opportunity to develop stronger patience and cultivate my love for others.

True life is full of interruptions. When I started praying for interruptions, God provided. He will provide opportunities for you, too. All you have to do is ask, and you will receive abundantly. However, when you ask God to strengthen your love and patience, don't expect it to be easy. In all honesty, it's going to be tough. But choose to do the right thing because of this, not in spite of it. It's the trials we think we can't make it through that bring us out the strongest.

As much as true life is full of interruptions, it is full of mistakes. Even when we mess up, His love goes on. Even when we fail, we are cared for. God understands. In all circumstances, His love takes action. Whatever happens, His love continues forever, the light that never fades.

Part Two:

In Christ Alone

In Christ Alone

by Keith Getty and Stuart Townend

In Christ alone, my hope is found,
He is my light, my strength, my song;
This Cornerstone, this solid Ground,
Firm through the fiercest drought and storm.
What heights of love, what depths of peace,
when fears are stilled, and strivings cease!
My Comforter, my All in All,
Here in the love of Christ I stand.

Eternal Hope:
My Hope is Found

I stepped outside at sunset, my favorite time to pray, on a beautiful, muggy Tennessee evening. Pink-orange bits of sky glowed from between massive clouds heavy with water. I started walking, figuring the rain would hold off. I prayed as I walked, talking to God. I'm sure the people watching from their windows thought I was weird. That's a fun bonus.

Lately, I'd been struggling. Everything was being canceled. Each time I clung to the hope that this event would take place or that this person would stay well, the exact opposite of what I hoped happened almost every time. But now *everything* had been canceled. *Everyone* was sick. When I was about halfway home, it started to sprinkle. I felt a drop splatter across my nose and began to sprint. As I raced against the rain, I laughed, a breathless huff.

Now the neighbors were definitely laughing.

As soon as I stepped onto my porch, the rain began in earnest. As I watched it fall, catching my breath, I had a sudden realization. I shouldn't trust in the hope of uncertainties. Events, camp, school, and even health are not guaranteed. I can't cling to the hope of good grades or late-night ice cream or negative COVID tests. I have no assurance in these things, no eternal promise.

But there is a hope that never fails. There lives a hope eternal. Instead of clinging to what I hoped God would *do* in my life, I realized I should just cling to *Him,* no matter what happened.

Worldly hope is dependent upon circumstances. Godly hope is a hope that comes from our Everlasting Light, Jesus. Amidst all we face, God is constant. He does not change; He will never leave us, forget us, or forsake us. He clings to us as we cling to hope in Him. He will never let go. If we lose hope, He grasps our hand tighter. If we forget, He reminds us of where our hearts should trust every day if that's what it takes. Day by day, God forgives us. Day by day, He answers prayers. Day by day, God reminds us of His glory. He keeps His promises without fail. God is our Everlasting Light and our eternal hope.

Hair wet with rain and face soaked with sweat, I smiled as I looked to the clouds above. "My hope is found," I breathed, a quiet certainty.

Still beaming, I slipped through the front door of my house where I could hear the pitter-patter of the rain all around me and feel the hope of God in my heart. I promised myself to never let go of it again. No matter what.

Hide Me Away

White water rafting is an unforgettable experience. The rushing water, the adrenaline kicking in as you try to stay in the boat. The mountains rising high on either side, full of trees and wildlife. It's incredible. But my favorite moment of a white rafting retreat with my church was not the rapids or the rush of the water. It wasn't the birds or the trees or the buzzing bees. It was a tender moment with someone I love dearly.

A little while after rafting, we all went down to the lake by our cabin to swim. When it was time to leave and we were putting our life jackets away, I realized I had forgotten my towel. We were all freezing as the temperature dropped, the sun sinking below the horizon. My boyfriend, Seth, asked if I wanted his towel, but I said no because I knew he was cold, too.

As we trekked back up a steep hill to the cabin together, I had my arms wrapped around myself because I was shivering. Without a word, Seth quietly came up behind me and wrapped the towel around my shoulders.

Surprised, I looked back, and he gave me a sweet smile. Then I asked, "What did you do that for? You need the towel, too."

He shook his head at me. "Well, if I had asked you again you would have said no. And I couldn't just let you be cold. I love you too much for that."

It was my turn to smile. All wrapped up in his towel, I stood on my tiptoes to give him a kiss on the cheek. Then we walked the rest of the way, admiring the splendor of the trees and lake surrounding us and our love for another.

In a similar way, sometimes we refuse help and comfort from God. He's holding out His hand to us, offering everything we need, and we choose not to accept it. However, just like my boyfriend placed the towel around my shoulders, God will take care of us even when we're too stubborn to admit we need help.

To live a life of everlasting light, we must allow God to take care of us.

For a long time, and sometimes even now, I struggled to allow anyone to comfort or help me, even God. I struggle and struggle and struggle until I absolutely have to have help. But every time, I could have saved myself a lot of pain by surrendering my pride and allowing myself to be taken care of. How have you struggled to accept comfort from God? What do you need to accept from God that He is offering you? Remember that God is reaching out His hand to help you. Will you take it?

I want to end with a poem I wrote while going through a difficult time at camp. It's called "He Hears Me":

He Hears Me

Thought safe was a place.
I guess I know now,
The only safe place
Is in God's arms.

I need Him to hold me,
A gentle hand brushing back my hair.
I need Him to whisper,
"Trust me, for I care."

Some things are easier to give
Than to receive,
And comfort
Falls from that tree.

Thought safe was a place.
I guess I know now,
The only safe place
Comes from breaking your walls down.

I won't give up,
Nor will I grow weary,
For through this long walk,
I know my Lord hears me.

Be Still and Know

At the start of soccer season, all players must get a physical and a concussion test to ensure they are healthy and able to play. We have to do all kinds of weird stuff like memorize a series of numbers, say the months of the year backwards, and stand on one foot for thirty seconds with our eyes closed.

Surprisingly, the most difficult test to pass is the latter: balance. Standing on one foot is not always easy, especially when you have to close your eyes and your legs are already exhausted from drills and running and workouts.

It was hilarious to watch as my teammates wobbled around while trying to pass the balance test. Honestly, you'd think we weren't soccer players.

When it was my turn, I took a deep breath, let my eyes drift closed, and raised my left foot off the ground. The breeze brushed my hair across my face, a soft whisper against my nose and cheeks. The warm sunlight coaxed a small smile onto my face.

I decided to use this time as a moment to find peace. I kept breathing, in and out, in and out, in and out. I thought of God and all the blessings in my life and the brush of the grass against my cleats. The sound of drills and whistles faded away as I allowed my mind to drift away from all that was worldly and step into the gentle stillness only God can offer.

My smile widened, my face splitting into a lopsided grin. All my anxiety fell away: all that was left was Jesus.

And then the timer went off and broke my focus, causing me to lose my balance and nearly go sprawling on the sidelines. I laughed at myself as I ran back onto the field, my heart still at peace despite my clumsiness.

When I look back on that quiet moment, I am reminded of the story of Jesus walking on the water in Matthew 14. The disciples were on a boat in the middle of the sea with the wind and waves beating against them. Earlier that day, Jesus had climbed up a mountain to spend some alone time in prayer. But as the disciples were fighting against the storm, Jesus walked on the water toward their boat. At first, they were terrified, thinking it was a ghost or a spirit, but then Jesus calmed them with kind words.

"But immediately Jesus spoke to them, saying, 'Take heart; it is I. Do not be afraid.'

And Peter answered, 'Lord, if it is you, command me to come to you on the water.'"

He said, 'Come.'

So, Peter got out of the boat and walked on the water and came to Jesus. But when he saw the wind, he was afraid, and beginning to sink he cried out, 'Lord, save me.'

Jesus immediately reached out his hand and took hold of him, saying to him, 'O you of little faith, why did you doubt?'

And when they got into the boat, the wind ceased. And those in the boat worshipped him, saying, 'Truly you are the Son of God.'" (Matthew 14:27-33 ESV)

In the same way, when I had an unwavering focus on God, my heart was at peace and my thoughts were still. I was walking on the water towards Jesus, all my concentration centered on Him. But like Peter losing focus because of the storm and beginning to sink, I lost focus when the timer buzzed, causing me to stumble.

To live a life of everlasting light, we have to live a life of eternal peace, not free from distractions (Satan will always be trying to tempt us), but *because* of them. When I stumbled, I jumped right back up and regained my focus on God. When Peter began to sink and Jesus pulled him back onto the boat, he instantly chose to focus on Jesus again.

Living a life of eternal peace is not about never falling. It's about getting back up stronger and closer to God each time you stumble, full of praise and stillness once more.

Use every moment you can to find peace. Take every opportunity you have to be still and know God is real. Let everything else fall away, open your heart, and allow God's gentle light to fill your body, mind, and spirit as you place your focus on Christ alone.

Everlasting Source

This past week was rough. My mom decided to take us to the beach for Thanksgiving; my best friend even tagged along. I was thankful for the vacation, but what I really wanted was to be with my whole family, eating at my grandparent's house. My uncle, who served in the Air Force, stopped by for a surprise visit while I was gone. I hadn't seen him in a year or two, and I'm not sure when I'll get to see him again. I found out that two of my friends were struggling with a lot of different things, including diagnosed anxiety and depression. I tried to comfort them, to be there for them in any way I could, but it didn't seem to be helping. I totaled my car, and it felt as if so much of my freedom was taken away: I had to depend on my parents again to get me everywhere I needed to be. And to top it all off, while we were at the beach, my best friend's mom contracted COVID-19. She got to stay with us until her mom got better, so she wouldn't get sick or have to quarantine. (That part, at least, was fun.)

While all this was happening, my parents and siblings were driving me absolutely insane. It wasn't really what they were doing: everything happening all at once was just so overwhelming. I was stressed and annoyed and not as kind as I should have been. I was irritated and losing my patience. I was hurting and couldn't handle it on my own.

And then I realized something. All this time, I had been drawing from my own well of love and patience and joy, a well that's limited because I'm human and I make mistakes. I had to make a decision: choose to give up or choose God.

I chose to start drawing love, patience, and joy from God, the everlasting source of light and goodness in all things, instead of pulling from my limited supply.

This decision changed my life. Suddenly I walked lighter, felt more at peace. My interactions with others changed completely, from *my* patience to God's *never-ending* patience. From *my* love to God's *eternal* love. From *my* joy to God's *unconditional* joy.

When we choose to pull from God's bottomless wealth of righteousness in our everyday interactions, we will experience His everlasting light like never before. Through a flow of kindness and wisdom, and a steady stream of forgiveness, we can learn to be slow to anger, resist temptation, and speak encouragement to others.

We can't encourage others if we don't fill our lives with unending patience, perfect love, and unshakable joy. We have to draw from God's everlasting source. If our well dries up, we have nothing left to give, but when we draw from God's well, the water will never run out.

If you find yourself becoming easily annoyed, caught in hatred, or imprisoned by sorrow, make the choice to draw patience, love, and joy from God, our everlasting source of all things pure and holy. Even in the darkness, His light will never be put out. Even in the storm, He won't let us lose our way. Even in the dry seasons of life, our hearts will always be filled if we draw from His well.

Abundant Provider

Waking up for school every morning at six a.m. is no fun. At the beginning of the school year, it's still dark outside as I'm getting ready, and I'm forced to miss the sunrise every morning. That is, until the time changes.

Once it changes in October and we gain an hour, I get to watch colors smear across the horizon in a myriad of warm hues as I wake up and prepare for the day. The beauty of the sunrise fills me with awe of God's power and creativity. He has the most incredible imagination there ever was, is, or will be. He created the earth and everything in it in perfect complexity and wisdom. Trees, flowers, blue skies. Rainy days, waterfalls, and still ponds. Even the birds singing a wistful tune, chirping, "The dawn is coming soon."

About a week before the time changes, however, I start to get discouraged. Waking up in darkness begins to weigh on me, the difficulties of everyday life and sin dragging me down. When I need it most, God sends hope in the form of a sunrise to start my day.

Whatever you may be facing, God will provide. He will take care of you.

A couple weeks ago, I hurt my hip at soccer practice. I told my mom and she told me it was fine. You know how moms are. So, I ignored the pain and continued working out and running, even though it hurt, even though I knew something was wrong. I guess I just thought it would simply go away eventually. That was my own fault. I should've listened to my body and gone straight to the doctor. But I didn't.

A couple days ago, I was racing some friends after school. The second I started running I knew it didn't feel right. About twelve feet down the track, my hip popped, and I stumbled. I nearly fell; when I stood up, I couldn't put any pressure on my left leg without piercing pain. My friends tried to help me, but I wouldn't let them carry me. I limped all the way to my car instead.

The x-ray and doctor's visit didn't help much. They couldn't tell us exactly what was wrong. All they could discern was that it wasn't the bone and that it was most likely a strained muscle. They prescribed crutches and pain meds for about a week.

At school on Monday, I was forced to hobble around on crutches and ask for help opening doors, carrying bags, and fixing my lunch tray. I hated the attention I had tried to avoid in the first place by ignoring the pain. But even more than that, I hated asking for help. I hated depending on others.

I was proud and hurting. I was afraid asking for help would make me seem weak.

In the same way, sometimes we sin and try to ignore the consequences. Maybe you didn't sin, but you're just struggling with something going on in your life. Please don't suffer in silence until you can't bear the pain anymore. Don't stretch yourself so thin that you snap.

As hard as it is, we have to surrender control to God. We can't do it on our own. We have to learn to depend on God to heal and stay healthy.

It's not easy, but if we want to live life to the full, we have to lay all our anxiety and fears and failures, all our pain, at the feet of the Savior. Only then can we walk light. Only then can we be free from sin.

Matthew 11:28-30 (NIV) says, "Come to me, all you who are weary and burdened, and I will give you rest. Take my yoke upon you and learn from me, for I am gentle and humble in heart, and you will find rest for your souls. For my yoke is easy and my burden is light."

As I struggled to use the crutches and perform activities that usually would've been a breeze, I became exhausted and anxious. I wanted to heal as quickly as possible so I could get back into the swing of things. However, my efforts to maintain my normal schedule without assistance slowed the healing. I began to get discouraged and a bit depressed.

Just like how God sent the sunrise to fill me with hope when I needed it most, He helped me realize this when I was tired and hurting: God's burden is light, and His heart is humble and gentle.

The burden of my injury and all that resulted from it was heavy, like the sin and pain in our lives. Our hearts are hardened and proud, the opposite of what Jesus has taught us to be. I knew I couldn't carry this burden on my own, and yet it still took me too long to ask for help.

I began to cry out to God, casting all my burdens on Him. In exchange for my worries, God gave me peace and mercy and joy. Not only did he make my burden light, as in taking an oppressive weight off my shoulders, but in a literal sense, He made my burden *light*.

Instead of bearing the weight of loss and sorrow and fear upon my heart, God filled me with a hope and a purpose. *My burden became light.* My burden became trusting in the Lord, leading others to eternal life through Jesus. My burden became learning to be humble and kind and gentle. My burden became living for God, and my dear friends, that is no burden at all. Being a light is my joy, not solely my duty.

When you surrender your life to God and cast all your burdens onto Jesus, who cares for you deeply and passionately, you will no longer be pinned down by discouragement. You will be set free. Your burden will be light, and you will be completely free.

To live a life of everlasting light, we have to live life to the full, and that means surrendering to God and trusting that He will provide. It means letting go of our pride and humbling ourselves as God has commanded. It means casting our cares on to God in prayer and making our burden light.

Will you stop suffering in silence and ask God for help or continue to live held back by your pain?

Two weeks after visiting the doctor, I was able to walk without crutches and with relatively little pain. I hadn't been able to go for a sunset prayer walk for a while because of my leg, so you can imagine my joy at finally being able to bask in the sinking sun as I spoke to my Savior and best friend.

Walking was still a bit difficult for longer distances, and every once in a while, I would feel a sharp pang in my hip. This whole time I had been scared I wouldn't be able to run or play soccer or work out again. A major block to my healing was mental. I would overthink every step, asking myself, "Will it hurt if I step this way? I don't want to trip over anything. It *hurts*. I need… I need help."

The whole purpose of going for a walk was to pray and refocus, but I was worried and distracted. Once I realized I needed help overcoming my fear, I began to pray. "Eyes on God, eyes on God. Eyes on God, eyes on God." As I kept repeating this, my anxiety eased, and I stopped overthinking every move.

When we keep our eyes on God instead of our fears and worries, His everlasting light becomes more evident in our lives. When we focus on what good and eternal things God has provided for us, sin and temptation fall away from our minds. But before we can trust God with our burdens, we have to accept that we need help. We have to choose to trust God, or allow our weaknesses to overwhelm us.

Jesus always made the decision to trust in God. In Matthew 26, Jesus went to a place called Gethsemane to pray. He was preparing to be crucified so that all of us, everyone who will ever live, is living, or has lived, could be free from sin. Crucifixion was the most humiliating and painful death possible during the time Jesus lived. The convicted were lashed with a whip, beaten, and then *nailed* to a cross. They died only when they could no longer lift themselves up to take an excruciating breath. Jesus, *a perfect sacrifice*, suffered the cross so that *we* could be free from sin. He suffered so that *we* could live. Don't ignore His sacrifice by living in the wrong way, full of pride and anger.

Jesus knew all this was going to happen and yet He remained faithful. If you knew you would endure this same pain for the name of the Lord, would you still trust in God's plan? Would you still trust that He will provide?

When Jesus was facing a difficult situation, He prayed. But He also allowed his friends to encourage Him. Our Savior knew He couldn't face this alone, and He trusted God and his friends to help Him through.

When you are discouraged, choose to live life to the full, a life that can only be gifted by God, the everlasting Provider. When you're stuck in the darkness, choose a life filled with everlasting light, free from sin and filled by Jesus. Choose God. When you are lost, choose the One who will take your pain and turn it into something beautiful. Choose the Savior who will bear your struggles and make your burden light.

God used a strained muscle to teach me how to surrender to Him and ask for help, to teach me how to be humble. God sends a sunrise every morning to show that He is taking care of us. God will provide. He will provide. Don't let your pride or pain get in the way of following Jesus. Choose to surrender. Choose to ask God and your friends for help. Choose God every time because His light will never go out.

Whenever you catch yourself stumbling, whisper, "Eyes on God, eyes on God. Eyes on God, eyes on God," and watch all your fears flee in the face of His everlasting goodness as your burden becomes light.

Unbroken Wonder

There are too many grownups who have lost the sense of childlike wonder that pervaded their world and made it glow in their early years of life. How many grownups do you know who catch fireflies before dinner on a humid summer night? How many adults do you know who watch the sunset each day, simply to see the colors? Do you know any adults who still wish on shooting stars?

A lot of the time, adults lose wonder because they start asking *why* too much. Knowing why fireflies glow, why the sun sets in a myriad of colors, and how the stars hang in the ceiling of the sky takes away the intriguing mystery, the pull of the unknown. They eventually reach a point where they feel like they know everything, and their curiosity dissipates. It happens to almost everyone. Knowing why everything is the way it is, how everything works, and what exactly all things are takes away the magic. It becomes more and more difficult to remember how to laugh, how to play, how to dance like nobody's watching.

So maybe instead of asking why all the time, we should just close our eyes and thank God for the wonders of this world, thank Him for the mysteries and miracles and magic. Instead of obsessing over answers, we should let God speak to us, guide us. Instead of snipping their imaginations, we should listen to the children around us; learn from them. They possess the purest kind of wonder.

Matthew 18:3 (ESV) says this, "… Truly, I say to you, unless you turn and become like children, you will never enter the kingdom of heaven."

Whether it's a terrible mistake, getting fired from a job, or failing to reach a goal, something causes our wonder to break. But God works in a completely different way than the world. If you let Him, He will take the things that break our wonder and turn them into things that astonish us. Things we can only gape at in surprise, amazement, adoration. He will transform us from tired, stressed adults to lively, wonder-filled children.

It's amazing to believe that out of all the marvels of this world, God created us to be His most beautiful creation. There is good in everything. There is beauty in everyone. Wonder is about finding the light in other people, finding God in them—always choosing to see the good. Always choosing to be amazed by His work in our lives and the people we have the pleasure to know and the places we'll go.

I want you to think about this as you prepare to pray to the Father: picture all moments in your childhood that made you curious, awed, or pleasantly surprised. Bring them to life in your mind. Use all your senses. What do you see? What do you hear? What do you feel, taste, smell? Remember these moments and then thank God for them. Ask Him to help you remember them the next time you are wrestling with something.

Wonder is about recognizing God in His creation, whether it be people, places, or moments. When I look back on my life, there are so many times in which I simply had to close my eyes and thank God for filling me with awe.

At fall camp, on a prayer walk through the changing wood, red leaves cascading from the treetops, the trail worn from many young feet, a cool breeze and warm sunlight on my skin. The smell of damp leaves and earth saturating the world around me, near-silence as the sun dipped the world into gold, a quiet hush consuming all life as everything but the sound of my soft steps on the ground and God whispering to my heart fell away.

Pouring my heart out during lights-out singing beneath the old wooden pavilion as stars shined bright upon the world, everything else dark, reminding me that God is the only true everlasting light. The bees slowing their sleepy buzz as the grasshoppers and cicadas began their nighttime lullaby. Grabbing the hands of friends and strangers as we stood up to finish our worship with one last song. A moment of charged silence before the prayer, everyone so awed at the beautiful, powerful praise of God we had just created together that nobody wanted to speak, interrupting the peaceful stillness of knowing God is in your midst.

Sprinting across the soccer field to the bathhouse after announcements to reach the showers first, pushing as fast as I could go, the stars a blur above me, the ground flying by beneath my feet. Nothing holding me back, laughing as I thanked God for this glorious moment of freedom.

Listening to a lesson delivered by the lake, the grass scratching my legs, mosquitoes biting my arms, heat making my head spin… And then it all fell away. My mind was entirely focused on Jesus, remembering the many times He had taught by a body of water. Wistfully wishing I could have been there, could've heard the voice of my Savior in the flesh, I imagined the taste of sea salt in the air, taking Jesus's hand, and following Him as the disciples did.

Laying on the soccer field in a time of midnight prayer, arms propped beneath my head, heart open to God, tears streaming down my face, forming warm dots on my t-shirt. Standing up, and walking away forever changed, choosing to encourage others, choosing to be a light.

Crossing over to my friends after a powerful devotional, embracing them, and walking to a quiet spot to talk. Feeling my burdens lessen as we shared and prayed for one another.

Flying on a plane for the first time I can remember, the clouds a misty array of white just outside my tiny window. Admiring the sky, noticing how my ears popped, and striking up conversations about the Good News with my neighbor. Relishing one moment of suspended-in-the-air calm before the pilot announced we were starting our descent.

Sitting next to a man from South Africa on a flight to Houston on the way to Nicaragua. Talking for almost the whole two hours about our lives, our stories, our faith. Sharing wisdom and what life in our homes was like. Learning that he was going home to see his wife and kids after several months of working in the United States. Saying goodbye as the plane landed and we pulled our carry-ons down from the cargo area. The man telling me he would not forget me, that he hoped we would meet again if I ever traveled to South Africa.

Sleeping on a paper-thin mattress with bats and rats scuttling in the ceiling above my head in Nicaragua. Not caring because I was focused on God and adventure and loving those around me. Walking on the black sand beaches, feeling God's presence in the mounting waves and setting sun.

Stepping out of the airport into the muggy air, startled by the sudden change in temperature.

Passing humbling volcanos on the road to León. Taking in the greenest grass, the bluest sky, the kindest eyes in the people I've ever seen. Getting to know them and loving them even before I knew their names.

Speaking Spanish with the people I met and making a friend, a kindred spirit: a beautiful soul who is so mature and wise for her age. A girl who speaks excellent English even though she doesn't realize how good she is.

Drinking café con miel for the first time. The rich sweetness of the honey mixed with milk against the bitter coffee created the perfect flavor. Oh, how I miss the café con miel!

Wandering the streets of the town square, visiting a towering cathedral, and shopping in the small booths set up on the sidewalks. Buying a floppy hat and later realizing I couldn't put it in my suitcase without crushing it. Wearing it all the way home, through two flights and two long car rides. It was winter in Tennessee. You should've seen the funny looks I got in my floppy summer hat and big warm coat. Laughter spilled from my lips at the absurdity of it. What? I couldn't help it!

Hugging the children at the school in Nicaragua as they graduated to their next year of education. Pride for them swelling in my heart, recognizing their determination and resilience, from the smallest child to the oldest woman.

Praying and thanking God like never before for the black sand beaches and kindhearted people and the glory of His Word and creation.

Having the opportunity to help Nicaragua in many unique ways from home, even when I couldn't travel there.

Growing closer to my parents and to God through helping others and sharing adventures.

Taking part in my mom and stepdad's and dad and stepmom's weddings. Rejoicing that they found love again, that light shined in their lives and smiles again, even though it wasn't always easy having four parents and two little siblings.

The day my little sister was born and my grandfather, always with his Diet Dr. Pepper in hand, came to surprise me and drive me to the hospital from camp so I could be there. And not knowing what exactly I was getting into.

When my little brother was born and still not knowing what I was getting into.

Thinking about the first time my siblings asked me about God. The biggest smile split my face as I did my best to explain in a gentle voice, holding their hands and kissing their foreheads as they ran off to play, ever curious and ever getting into trouble.

The mouth-watering smell of chocolate chip cookies in the oven and the satisfaction of eating them once they've cooled down.

The night before Christmas, the whole world waiting in anticipation to see what gifts will be sitting under the tree the next morning. The silence when everyone else in the house is asleep, but you're too excited to close your eyes. Celebrating the birth of Jesus, offering thanks for His sacrifice by praising Him and giving to others as He would have done.

Falling asleep with the hope of snow the next day and waking up to a winter wonderland. Icicles frozen mid-drip along the rims of a house blanketed in white and along the bottom of cars parked outside. A sharp breeze and muted sun. The howling wind. Quiet.

Watching many people be baptized. In the pool at camp, in a lake on retreats, in the baptistry at church… Each one is unique, carrying a special God-given story to share with those who long for God's appearance in their lives.

My own baptism, the weight of sin washed away as my dad pulled me up from the water feeling lighter than ever before.

My dad giving me my first Bible with a plush doll for Easter, reading and highlighting verses I couldn't yet fully comprehend but loving them, nevertheless. I knew they came from the same God who created the many beauties of this world; I wanted to make a friend of Him, the One my parents always told me about at home, the Savior my teachers taught me about in Bible class. The magnificent Creator who paints the sky each night and makes the fireflies glow.

Biking to watch the sunrise on the beach with my best friend on vacation, enjoying God's beauty together, choosing to wonder. Marveling at the many jellyfish swimming in the waters below the pier later that night while eating peanut butter frozen yogurt topped with strawberries. Ziplining by the shore on a later trip, the ocean a vast blue beneath and before us.

Leaping for the chance to take a sunset prayer walk at every opportunity. Stopping on the front porch before I open the front door, closing my eyes, and taking a moment to simply listen. A breeze, wind chimes, rustling leaves, cars passing by, birds chirping, squirrels scurrying up a branch, the day softly seeping into night. And a soft tapping on my heart. God.

Reading a book on my own for the first time, fully understanding what was written. My eyes widening as I formed the words without help from my parents, giddy with what I had accomplished.

Falling into a book at the end of a long day, allowing the story to take me away to a place of marvels and dreams. The smell and the feel of the pages between my fingers as I glide through chapter after chapter.

Writing my own stories and writing this book during the off moments of busy everyday life, an adventure and a joy unlike any other. An all-consuming peace through Christ Jesus. Relief.

Finding still moments throughout the day to slip my eyes closed and pray, dream, or remember whatever may be on my heart.

Do you know what most of these moments have in common? Stillness. Silence. Quiet. If we aren't quiet, we won't be able to hear God's whisper.

The story of Elijah on the mountain in 1 Kings 19 once again reminds us God speaks in quiet whispers, not in winds, earthquakes, and fire. Elijah listened and heard God because he chose to be still and patient. He was passionate in His relationship with the Lord; Elijah knew who the Lord was: He recognized Him when He passed by. It's in the gentle-whisper moments that we will feel God's everlasting light of hope and amazement fill our hearts the most, soft but mighty.

Fiery Furnace

G od is the only one who can comfort us and help us let go of fear. We can't do it on our own. However, while God is where our refuge and help ultimately come from, He sends friends to guide and encourage us.

In the book of Daniel, Meshach, Shadrach, and Abednego were three God-fearing best friends. They were constantly uplifting one another, taking a stand together. When King Nebuchadnezzar ordered them to worship an idol, they refused and were punished by being thrown into a blazing hot fiery furnace.

But because of their faith, God did not allow them to be burned, and He saved them from the fire. Then all the men present, including the king, worshipped and praised the one true God.

Meshach, Shadrach, and Abednego could never have survived these trials without God, but they also never would have made it without each other.

Daniel 11:35 (NCV) says, "Some of the wise ones will be killed. But the hard times must come so they can be made stronger and purer and without faults until the time of the end comes. Then, at the right time, the end will come."

We have to face trials, like the three friends and the fiery furnace, and follow God no matter what it means risking, because it will make us stronger in the Lord.

I want to share a journal entry with you about a time in my life I wouldn't have made it through without a friend. Thank you, God, and thank you, Mia, for being there to help me when I needed it most.

God,   1-8-2020

Lately I've been thinking about a childhood memory. I was about seven or eight when our youth minister took a group to an awesome cave to explore. We entered through the gates with a sign that said "NO TRESPASSING." I had no idea what that meant at the time, but I thought it sounded like something an explorer would do, so I pretended I was on an adventure. We parked the old vans and hiked a little ways until we came to a fork in the road.

To our left was a small stream of water which a guy in our youth group drank out of. My uncle snorted, "There's no telling what all has peed in that water."

The guy took another gulp of water and deadpanned, "I am one with nature." And then followed our youth minister as he shimmied up into the cave under a low rock army-style.

The kids, teenagers, and smaller adults followed after them. Everybody else trekked up a hill to enter the cave from a bigger spot.

The cave was dark and echoing and seemed to hold so much wisdom, so many secrets. I gently ran a hand along the wall as I slowly crept deeper into the darkness. My hand brushed something cold, and I jumped back, snapping my head to where I thought a bat or a snake or a bug was trying to kill me.

After I calmed down enough to realize it wasn't a spider, I saw a glimmer of white and cautiously reached out to skim my fingers against its edges.

My aunt came up behind me and whispered, "Do you know what that is?" I shook my head. "It's a crystal." She gently took my hands in her own and helped me unlodge it from the rock. It released with a resounding crack.

I held it tightly in my little hands before walking on. After more exploring, we reached a large, cleared area where we sat down to ensure nobody had gotten lost. When everyone was accounted for, our youth minister announced that we would be turning out all the lights and singing praise to God.

One by one, all the flashlights began to blink out. Tentatively, I turned mine off with tears in my eyes. I was scared, but my friend Mia held my hand as we sang praise to God, the words consuming the space to create a lulling, ethereal hum. She held my hand as we prayed. She held my hand until I wasn't afraid anymore. I could sense a shared feeling of awe at God's creation connecting everyone who had praised Him in the dark.

On our way out, Mia discovered what we believed to be a worm fossil... Then she accidentally broke it a few minutes later. Our youth minister nearly got his head taken off by a bat, and somehow a boy a few years younger than me cut his head open on a rock. His mom threw some glue on there and the kid toughed it out. (That family is notorious for their toughness.)

My last memory of my adventure was my cousin telling me that once eye boogers touch someone they NEVER go away. However fun and interesting all these other things were, the one thing I will never forget is praising God in the dark with a true friend by my side.

—Lily K. Lewis

Best Friend

In the middle of my seventh-grade year, I switched schools. While I had nothing against the school I was at, I knew the other school was a better option for me; I could feel God tapping on my heart. So, I talked to my parents, I prayed, and the next semester I started at a new school.

During the Christmas break before I switched schools, I caught the flu and pneumonia. I was miserable for a few weeks and still tired months after that. Heading into a new school feeling exhausted all the time was terrible. It was harder to make friends, harder to laugh, and harder to focus on my work when I could feel the phantom heaviness of pneumonia pressing down on my chest. Although I had friends, I never felt like I entirely fit in.

Eighth-grade year passed, and it was pretty much the same as seventh-grade year, although I was less tired and more myself again. I made more friends and we shared so many fun times. I was invited to birthday parties and sleepovers and movies. It was a lot of fun. But still, I knew I stood out; I knew I was still searching for something more.

During the summer before high school, my mom asked me to pray for her to find a friend. She felt like I did—as if nobody quite understood her. She needed someone to help her grow closer in her relationship with God. I needed the same thing. And so, I prayed. And, of course, God provided.

My mom is a sixth-grade social studies teacher, and she's really good at what she does. I love seeing her passion for teaching, even on the days when things are hard. One of her favorite things to teach is writing. And, boy, let me tell you, those kids come out of her class writing the most beautiful summaries anybody ever saw an eleven-year-old write. She's helped me a lot with my writing, too, and I'm incredibly thankful for that.

A couple of years ago, my mom started teaching with a man named Aaron Stratton. It was his first time teaching and his wife Kalyn's third year teaching. My mom helped them out when they had questions or needed tips. The first time I met Kalyn was toward the end of my ninth-grade year. I ran into her at a church I was visiting in the area, and I had no idea who she was, but she knew me from a picture she saw in my mom's classroom. I was really confused the until she told me who she was, and we shared a good laugh.

A couple weeks after that, the Strattons came to visit our house. At first, I didn't realize what God was up to. I didn't realize He was answering my prayer. They started coming to dinner more and more often, even coming over to hang out, exchange books with my mom, and go swimming at our neighborhood pool. We would also hang out at their house. I even ran into Aaron at a restaurant. It seemed like God was placing the Strattons in our path around every turn, trying to make us see He was answering our prayer.

The Strattons lived on the other side of town, about thirty minutes away from everything. They were searching for a new home, something spacious and closer to everywhere they needed to go.

For some reason, my mom has a habit of finding people houses they love. The Strattons were no exception. It just so happened that the perfect house for the Strattons was in our neighborhood, one street down and a two-minute car ride away. Who could have planned that but God?

The house didn't have a FOR SALE sign, but while my mom was walking one day, she noticed the house was under some serious construction. She decided to walk up and ask about it. I don't know what drove her to do this. Maybe it was curiosity, maybe it was a whim, but I like to think it was God tapping on her heart, that she said yes to what He was asking of her.

It turned out the house was, in fact, being almost completely remodeled. It was within the Stratton's price range, and it had everything they were looking for. My mom showed it to them, and they loved it. They talked to the owner and the house was sold before the FOR SALE sign went up. They moved in a few weeks later.

Kalyn and Aaron are always a joy to be around, always bringing an abundance of laughter and sarcasm to any conversation they enter. They love musicals, and they introduced me to the soundtracks of *Phantom of the Opera* and *Anastasia*, two of my favorites now. Kalyn, like my mom, is an excellent baker. The flow of sweets from our house to theirs, and vice versa, is as constant as the flow of books. I love playing disc golf with them, and I appreciate Aaron working with me to reach my full potential. He taught me many techniques of throwing discs and worked with me often until I improved. He is a wonderful teacher, whether the topic be social studies, disc golf, or making meringues.

In the same way, Kalyn helped me a lot in my spiritual life. When I went on a kayaking trip with her and a family we had reconnected with through the Strattons, we had a great conversation about God that I always look back on and smile. When they moved into their new house, I helped them arrange all their bookshelves. One of the things my mom loves most about Kalyn is that she isn't judgmental: she can always be open with her. She loves sharing recipes, talking over cups of coffee (the Strattons both have their own mugs at our house), and teaching with them. She often talks about what an awesome teacher Kalyn is and how they help each other a lot. She also loves how hospitable they are, a trait my mom values highly.

Since the Strattons moved in, they have been more than dear family friends. They helped us reconnect with some old friends we lost touch with, and my mom found a best friend in Kalyn. She was exactly what my mom needed. I prayed for my mom to find a friend, a true friend, and God provided. He provided for me, too.

In ninth-grade Lifetime Wellness class, I met Hannah Lyons, the girl who would become my best friend, for the first time. She had thick brown hair she almost always wore in a ponytail and wacky socks like the ones I loved to wear. She was constantly smiling and brightened every room with her laughter. She loves sweets (*all* the sweets) and can always chow down on a burrito, her favorite food. She's a beast at volleyball, and like me, very competitive in card games. She's always joking around but knows when it's time to be serious, even though we know neither of us can keep a straight face if the other is in the room. She always encourages me and asks about my day, which has always meant a lot to me. She offers an open ear when I'm struggling, gives really good hugs to make me feel better, and shares how she can relate to my situation, how she understands what I'm going through. She listens when I want to bounce an idea off someone for a project or when I want to read her a chapter of the book I'm working on. She always stops for anything associated with raising money for children's hospitals, having lost her younger cousin to cancer, and offers a kind smile, even though I know it hurts her to think about it. She engages people who are hurting and shares how much her cousin meant to her family, comforting and encouraging them. Hannah has been such a blessing, a greater one than I can even explain.

I prayed for God to give me a friend, and He sent a best friend, the best best friend I ever could have asked for. But she wasn't just my best friend. As the Strattons had become a part of our family, so did Hannah. And I became a part of her family, too. Now we're all very close, always laughing together, uplifting one another. Through her, and the Strattons, God provided the one thing I had been searching for all along: friends who would draw my family nearer to Him.

The thing I love most about our friendship is that we can talk about God and other spiritual things. Hannah's devotion to her faith inspires me every time she shares something God has taught her; I can't help the swell of pride for my beautiful light of a friend that sweeps over my heart. She inspires me to be a better Christian. She inspires me to be a better friend.

We have so many memories together. Getting accidentally caught in a political parade on the road to my house, going on vacation together, waking up early and riding our bikes to the beach to watch the sunrise. Walking and talking through my neighborhood, tackling each other into a pile of autumn leaves, and laughing so hard we can't breathe. Throwing Christmas, Halloween, and Valentine's Day parties with our other friends. Baking and cooking and going shopping. (We have a habit of finding the other something they never would have picked out for themselves but end up loving anyway.) Singing at the top of our lungs and knowing all the same songs. Watching movies and creating handshakes and making silly faces at each other during class. Going for hikes on nearby trails. Giving each other gifts for "Gal"entine's Day and randomly bringing her cookies because I know how much she loves them. Having my first car accident when she was in the passenger seat. She knew exactly what to do when I had no idea what the next step would be. Collaborating with her parents to completely redo her room and getting to see her reaction when we surprised her with it on Christmas morning. Through her, God taught me how to laugh again, how to really laugh, after being sick and tired for so long. I can't thank Him enough, but I will try every day by being the best friend I can possibly be for Hannah.

One night, Hannah surprised me while we were having a sleepover. We always pray before we go to sleep, taking turns on who says the prayer, and tonight it was her turn. Except this time, she did a little something different. She pulled out a book and began to read from Psalm 63:1-8 (ESV):

"O God, you are my God; earnestly I seek you; my soul thirsts for you; my flesh faints for you, as in a dry and weary land where there is no water. So I have looked upon you in the sanctuary, beholding your power and glory. Because your love is better than life, my lips will praise you. So I will bless you as long as I live; in your name I will lift up my hands. My soul will be satisfied as with fat and rich food, and my mouth will praise you with joyful lips, when I remember you upon my bed, and meditate on you in the watches of the night; for you have been my help, and in the shadow of your wings I will sing for joy. My soul clings to you; your right hand upholds me."

Emotion dripped from her every word, and I saw God's light flash brighter in that moment. I could hear that she believed every word she spoke, and it made my own belief even stronger. I closed my eyes and listened, feeling the prayer with her as she spoke, opening my heart to God, praising Him. Truly, He was with us that night and every day before and after that fantastic prayer. I didn't think my love for Hannah could grow any stronger, but every day it only grows for her and the Strattons and all those around me. I prayed for God to send me a friend, and He provided a best friend. And through her, He taught me how to love others like Jesus loved His friends.

The friendships based on Christ alone—those are the ones that last. To live a life of everlasting light, we need friends who help us in our walk of faith, friends who encourage us, inspire us, and understand us. I want you to think about this: are the friends you have now friends who bring you closer to God? Or is God tapping on your heart to pray for a deeper friendship, one that will really satisfy you?

It is my sincere hope that each and every one of you, dear readers, will learn to accept who you are and that you find a friend who helps you grow closer to God. I am praying for you. In Christ alone can you accomplish this. Prayer and reading your Bible will help you see how God is working in your life. Developing a more intimate relationship with God and with your friends will help you to see Him, and others, more clearly.

Find the friend who brings you a studying care package when you can't hang out because you have a big test coming up. Find the friend you can always talk to, always trust. Find the friend who brings you closer to God and your life will be filled with everlasting light like never before. And when God provides him or her, hold on tight and never let go.

Part Three:

True Life

My Task

by Tennessee Ernie Ford

To love someone more dearly ev'ry day
To help a wand'ring child to find his way
And smile when evening falls
This is my task
To follow truth as blind men long for light
To do my best from dawn of day till night
And answer when He calls
This is my task

The Living Dead

I am so not a fan of horror movies. I've never enjoyed them. I even make excuses not to watch them during the month of Halloween. When I was younger, I only had to worry about avoiding scary movies in October. But nowadays, there are scary movies and TV shows released *every month of the year*. One of the monsters that scares me the most is zombies. There's a popular show called *The Walking Dead* that my dad loves to watch. He's the kind of guy that likes to watch anything he deems as "manly." It seems like every week he's watching some new spy show or war movie or Viking saga. One of his favorite genres, and one of my least favorites, is the zombie apocalypse. About a year ago, he watched all ten seasons of *The Walking Dead*. Although I wouldn't have believed it at the time, the show ended up teaching me something about Jesus.

So often, we walk through life without knowing what's really going on. We stumble and struggle to our feet in an endless cycle of monotonous days and repeated mistakes. We have everything laid out in front of us, but we are too lazy to take action. God is speaking, but we refuse to listen. God is showing us His glory, but we refuse to see. We know what is right, but we refuse to proclaim the truth. We know what is right, but we refuse to stand up and walk. We're like zombies, zombies who, rather than allowing "brains" to consume their minds, allow sin and social media and grades to take over our lives.

If we focus on anything but God, we are reduced to zombies. We lack purpose and wander around aimlessly in search of something that will satisfy us. Maybe your "brains" are sports and parties and drugs. Maybe they're sex and lies and alcohol. We chase after them mindlessly, forgetting that our purpose comes from the Lord. We fall deeper and deeper into sin until we don't remember how to do anything but worry and question and fear. We become like the walking dead.

If we want to find everlasting life, we must leave our "brains" behind. A life without following Jesus is not really living. We have to place Jesus first and set everything else aside. In Exodus, the Israelites continually turned away from God and worshipped idols. They forgot how great He was, the miracles He had performed in the past, and His promises for the future. They were lost in the wilderness for forty years, searching for something to save them. And even though God sent daily reminders that He was with them, they refused to acknowledge Him.

At night, God appeared in a column of fire to light the way. During the day, God appeared as a column of cloud to guide their steps. Every moment, God was with them, and each day God provided food from the sky and prevented their bodies from aching and their clothes from tearing. No matter how far they traveled or what they faced, God gave them strength. When they reached a place they couldn't cross alone, God parted the waters so they could walk on dry land and escape from the enemy.

Maybe you're in a place you can't cross alone. Maybe you're addicted or lost or just feeling alone. Whatever you're facing, whatever "brains" you're chasing after, God will be there to part the waters and lead you back to

Him. In the midst of waves crashing around us, seas raging against our minds, God reminds us of who He is by giving us a dry path to safety. Exodus 14:14 (NIV) says, "The Lord will fight for you; you need only to be still." Surrender the "brains" you are chasing to God, and He will part the waters and fight the battle for you. You only have to choose to take the dry land.

When we choose God over everything else, we are ready to start our new life, our true life. Our everlasting life. You can't receive true life by chasing "brains" like pornography or cigarettes. Everlasting life can only come from God and be given by God. God sent Jesus, His only Son, as a perfect sacrifice so that we might *live*. Jesus did not sin and did not deserve to die, let alone suffer at the hand of unbelievers and endure being nailed to the cross. And yet, He chose to die for us so that we could have eternal life. But how can we receive this everlasting life? To receive eternal life in Christ Jesus, we must be baptized.

Acts 2:38 (NIV) says, "Peter replied, 'Repent and be baptized, every one of you, in the name of Jesus Christ for the remission of your sins. And you will receive the gift of the Holy Spirit.'"

When we are baptized, we are made pure and whole. We are forgiven and made new. The "brains" we used to chase fall away, and God's call to share the Good News about Jesus fills our hearts and minds. To live a life of everlasting light, we must be baptized and share the Good News about Jesus.

Everyone is called to be baptized. No matter what mistakes you've made or what "brains" you've chased in the past, God wants you to have eternal life. God wants you to be with Him in heaven one day. There are no restrictions or cut-offs for baptism. Everyone is called to be baptized: people from all races, genders, backgrounds, and countries. *You* are called to be baptized. God forgives everyone; God forgives all you have done.

Matthew 28:19-20 (NIV) says, "'Therefore go and make disciples of all nations, baptizing them in the name of the Father and of the Son and of the Holy Spirit, teaching them to obey everything I have commanded you. And surely I am with you always, to the very end of the age.'"

In the same way that everyone is called to be baptized, everyone is called to share their testimony and guide others to baptism and discipleship. By sharing the story of how you went from chasing after "brains" to following Jesus, you can inspire others to do the same.

Don't live life as a zombie anymore. Cry out to God to deliver you, and He will show you what true life looks like. Surrender your "brains" to God and be baptized. Share your story; share Jesus's story. Show others what everlasting life with Christ Jesus looks like. And when you find that eternal life, you will walk in everlasting light.

Leg Wrestling

I'm really good at leg wrestling. If you don't know what leg wrestling is, it's a game where two people lay side by side on the floor facing opposite directions. On the count of three, both people lock ankles and try to flip the other over. The one who gets flipped loses.

I've faced people who are bigger than me and faster than me and sometimes even stronger than me, and yet I've still won. The secret to winning a leg wrestle is catching the other person off guard. Even if they are stronger than you, you can beat them simply by flipping their leg before they have a chance to flip yours. If they are bigger than you, all you have to do is strike fast and strike without mercy.

The devil tempts us in a similar way. Satan knows we are stronger than Him. He knows that we could beat him if given the chance. So instead of waiting for us to slip up and give us a chance to recover, he flips our lives around without warning. Disaster can strike in an instant. We are hardly ever prepared for the phone call that a loved one passed away from a heart attack. We aren't prepared to hear the diagnosis or the failing grade or the lost hope. We aren't prepared for our lives to come crashing down around us, and Satan will take advantage of this *every single time.*

1 Peter 5:8 (NKJV) says, "Be sober, be vigilant; because your adversary the devil walks about like a roaring lion, seeking whom he may devour."

To win the fight against Satan, we must be vigilant and aware of what's happening around us. We have to find stillness in knowing God is with us through whatever life throws at us. *To be prepared, we have to be at peace.* To have steadfast hope in God's everlasting light we have to be prepared for it to *seem* dim sometimes. Emotions will cloud our vision, and grief will weigh on our hearts if we aren't prepared for trials. We must believe that God's promises, which do not change, are stronger than our emotions, which can shift constantly. We must be prepared for God's light to seem dim so that, through faith, we can remember His promises and know His light actually shines brighter in the darkness.

Car Crash

I got my very first car when I was fifteen. My parents allowed me to get my hardship license, which means that I was only allowed to drive to school and practice and home. I worked hard to earn my car. My grandfather cut us a deal. He told us he would either sell his car for five-hundred dollars, or we could do housework and earn it. My parents chose housework. My stepdad and I painted my grandparent's house while they were preparing to move. It was a lot of painting, but we still had a great time. A bonding experience for both of us, we joked as we climbed on ladders to reach the high walls, laughed when we had to fix a mistake, and shrieked as we threw balls of painter's tape at each other. It took a long time and a lot of effort to complete, but admiring the finished product made us both proud of what we had accomplished. I was also proud that I had earned my car, with some help from my stepdad.

My grandfather's car was a blue 2003 Saturn with over two hundred thousand miles on it. It was scratched, and the paint was chipping off, but it was mine and I had earned it. And now that it was mine, it was time to choose a name.

I examined the car's exterior with a thoughtful expression, walking in a slow circle around the vehicle. I carefully opened the door and sat in the driver's seat. My stepdad, Nolan, hopped into the passenger side.

I tenderly placed my hands on the wheel and looked down to appraise this, too. Right there, written in the middle of the steering wheel, was the word Saturn. I gasped and grabbed my stepdad's arm. I looked him dead in the eye with the biggest smile on my face and whispered, "Urnie." When he peered at me quizzically, I clarified, "The car's name is Urnie."

Then a grin split his face, and he chuckled while rubbing the back of his neck. "Well, kid, I definitely think the name fits." And so it was. The car's name was Urnie.

The next three months were some of the best of my life so far. About a month after I got Urnie, I was able to get my actual license because I turned sixteen. It was wonderful to drive around whenever I wanted, pick up friends, and get to places when I wanted to be there. I remember the first day I pulled up to school driving Urnie, with my red-rimmed sunglasses and music playing loud. I felt like the real deal. I have so many beautiful memories of Urnie. Truly, everything was great for those three months.

A couple nights before Thanksgiving, my best friend and I were in an accident. I was driving. We had a green light, but when I was in the middle of the intersection, a big truck turned left right in front of me. I slammed on the break and avoided hitting the truck or anybody else. I exhaled a sigh of relief. But then the trailer attached to the back of the truck came into view, and my car, which hadn't yet come to a complete stop, slammed into the very end of it.

The airbags deployed and the car spun out. Luckily, we didn't hit anybody else. Luckily, we didn't get hurt. However, the same couldn't be said for Urnie. Urnie was completely totaled. The whole front right side of the car was exposed; parts were scattered all across the street. The car was even smoking.

We called the police, and an ambulance came by to make sure everyone was okay. The truck driver was unharmed, and there was minimal damage to his trailer. The police showed up and took both sides of the story, asking witnesses what had occurred. It was freezing outside when my parents came, providing jackets and hugs to keep us warm.

The tow truck came, and I had tears in my eyes as the man swept up chunks of my car from the road and then loaded Urnie onto his trailer.

By the end of the night, the police hadn't officially determined whose fault it was. My parents drove us to the party we were heading to and then picked us up after. I prayed.

I was so anxious the following weeks, waiting for the official report. I knew it wasn't my fault, and the witnesses vouched on my behalf, but somehow doubt began to creep in. I questioned how fast I had been going, if I had done the wrong thing, what I could have done better. I worried about finding a new car if his insurance didn't cover the damage. I worried about getting to where I needed to be and suddenly being dependent on my parents again. It's a terrible feeling to taste freedom for such a short time and then have it ripped out of your hands.

I missed Urnie and all the wonderful memories I'd had with him. I missed picking up my friends for coffee and school and book shopping. I missed driving myself to church, Bible study, and Young Life Club. I missed being independent. I missed blasting my eighties rock music. I missed all of Urnie's scratches and scars and quirks.

And after the car crash, it was like one thing after another kept going wrong. I became more and more anxious as the days went by. My great-grandmother's sister died, and she was devastated. I kept praying. My best friend came to the beach with my family over Thanksgiving break; her mom got COVID while we were gone. She couldn't go home because she didn't want to risk getting sick, so she stayed with us for another two weeks until her mom was well. I kept praying. As soon as her mom was well, my dad and stepmom tested positive for COVID, and we had to quarantine again. I kept praying.

We missed Christmas parties and caroling and hanging out with friends. We even missed most of our final exams and would have to wait to take them in January after Christmas break. We couldn't even go Christmas shopping or visit family. In short, it was awful that we were in quarantine until a few days before Christmas. We still hadn't received the official police report for the car crash. Nevertheless, I prayed. Again, I kept getting more and more stressed, worried about every little thing.

And then a dear friend reminded me what a blessing quarantine is. It's a time to find stillness and refocus. It's an opportunity to do some things you normally wouldn't have the time to. It was a time to work on writing and read more books. It was a time to bake and write Christmas letters and decorate the house. It was a time to watch Hallmark movies with hot chocolate and laugh. It was a time to be with my family. It was a time to be with God, taking sunset prayer walks and meditating on His Word. It was a time to pray.

And as I was reminded of how wonderful quarantine had been in so many ways earlier in the year, not just because of the good moments but because of the struggles that made me stronger, I smiled. I fell to my knees and prayed. My anxiety slowly seeped away like the gentle thaw of sunshine after a long winter.

The next day, we received a call from the police station. My mom stepped out of the room to answer; the whole time they were talking my heart was beating *so* fast. I closed my eyes and called out to the Lord. I decided that no matter what happened, I would choose God. I dared to hope. My heart dropped when my mom came up to me with a neutral expression on her face. I braced for the bad news.

But then she smiled and gave me a big thumbs up. Immediately, I let out a sigh of relief and closed my eyes, thanking and praising God. We all hugged and laughed and celebrated. Not only had God had answered my prayer, but He gave me more than I had asked for.

For the old car my grandfather traded for helping with housework, we received a three-thousand-eighty-eight-dollar check from the insurance company for the damage done to Urnie. I was going to get a new car! I was going to be able to do all the things I had missed so much once again. Although I still missed Urnie, and no car could ever replace him, I was beyond happy that I would have my own car again.

From then on, quarantine overflowed with an abundance of joy. Not only had God healed my best friend's mom, but he healed my dad and stepmom, too. He comforted my great-grandmother in her mourning, shining light into her life again. My home was filled with unprecedented holiday cheer. My heart was open to God like never before. We shopped for gifts online and Facetimed friends. The stars were bright, and the sky was clear. We searched for a new car. Although this wasn't the holiday season I pictured, it was better than I had asked for. Not in spite of trials, but *because* of them. Continually, God answered my prayers. Continually, He reminded me not to be anxious. Continually, He taught me how to trust and to hope.

Psalm 126:5 (NIV) says this: "Those who sow with tears will reap with songs of joy." When times are dark and the season doesn't seem to be changing anytime soon, remember to choose joy, and it will be yours. Remember to thank God by finding the good in your situation and praising Him for it. Remember to pray.

As my heart overflowed with joy after receiving the good news about Urnie, I took a sunset prayer walk. The sky was beautiful, and the weather was warm, unusual for Tennessee in December. I thanked God over and over again, unable to fully express my gratitude for all this meant to me. My heart was light. There was no longer a weight of anxiety dragging me down.

Relief. That's what God had given me. Relief.

Relief from stress and worry and pain. Relief from anxiety and fear and grief…

Through these trials, He once again taught me how to walk light, how to hope, how to choose joy in all circumstances. He helped me focus on the good. He reminded me that He answers prayers. He provided.

Even when my mom tested positive for COVID, and I had to isolate for another fourteen days, even when my grandmother, aunt, and friends tested positive for COVID too, I prayed. I chose joy. I chose to praise God, to thank Him for this opportunity, rather than blame Him.

To live a life of everlasting light, we must be continually reminded of God's goodness and choose to trust in Him. We have to listen to what God is saying to us and remember the blessings He has given us. We have to keep praying.

I encourage you to bring all that you are struggling with before the Lord *right now*. I hope you will choose to throw off whatever weight is holding you back and allow God to fill you with relief and peace and light, no matter what you are facing, because God answers prayers. God is good and He will provide. True life is precious. Don't waste it by being negative and walking the wrong path. Choose God. Choose everlasting light.

Baby in the Snow

You won't believe what happened a few days later. We found the perfect car. God provided, and He provided in an absolutely wonderful way.

My stepdad was searching for a nice, used car online when he came across a red 2005 Solara. I remember gasping excitedly and clutching the back of his rolling chair as I leaned on it from behind him, staring at the computer screen with rows upon rows of cars in every color, style, and brand. The red car jumped out at me immediately. He clicked a button, and we discovered it was in perfect condition despite the 265,000 miles it had trekked; it was being sold from Missouri. He called the owner to discuss the car while I stood beside him, unable to keep still, so full of hope and excitement as I bounced from foot to foot. When he hung up, I looked up at him expectantly, and his face brightened into a smile. He said the car seemed perfect. It was shiny and smooth and lacked any complications, external or internal. We were willing to buy it, but there were a few obstacles standing in our way.

The owner lived in Missouri, so we would have to drive over four hours to get the car. We needed another adult to go with us because my parents didn't want me driving alone for that long on unfamiliar roads in icy weather. These were all minor complications, easily solved. However, one major obstacle remained... We still hadn't received the check from the insurance company. We didn't have the money to buy the car without it, so we had to wait. The owner kindly agreed to hold the car for us until it came in the mail.

But the days dragged by; there was no sign of the check coming. Every day, I would bound to the mailbox to see if it had arrived. Every day, I would pray, but there was yet to be any sign of the check.

About a month and a half had passed since the wreck, and still no sign of the check which would cover my new car and pave the path to freedom once more. I prayed that if God wanted me to have this car, He would provide a way. I prayed that if this car was not in His plan, I would wait patiently for the right one to come along. I began to pray for *patience* in finding the right car and receiving the check rather than just receiving the check and buying a new car.

Well, the check from the insurance company still hadn't come in, but my parents received a stimulus which they decided to use to buy me the car. Then, they used the insurance check for other things. I agreed immediately, seeing God at work. My cheeks hurt from smiling as I thanked and hugged them and ran off to share the news with my best friend. Hopefully, the car would be mine in only a few short days. It seemed like God was still answering my prayers for interruptions to teach me patience. It seemed like I would never get the car because of what muddied up the path, but every time I chose to be patient, He provided a way past the obstacle.

We tried to cash the check, but all the banks were closed for a holiday. It was the only day we could go, so the owner agreed to let us pay over

Venmo. One of my stepdad's close friends joined us on the trip to Eureka, Missouri to drive one of the cars back home.

As we drove, I prayed that if this was the right car, I would give thanks, and if it wasn't, I would rejoice because I knew God had an even better plan coming. I chose to say yes to God even if it meant saying no to what I wanted. I trusted He had something better planned.

When we arrived at the meeting spot just outside of St. Louis, the car was all I had imagined it would be and more. Any qualms about whether this was the right car or not, if this was really what God wanted for me, were silenced when it began to snow. The flurries fell gently, melting as they graced my skin, hair, eyelashes. There was a softness, a whisper, upon the air. A warmth somehow in the sky, easing the mall parking lot into wonder. God's presence was there with me, with us.

Through the snow, I knew God was saying, "Yes, Lily. You have been rewarded for your patience. This is My gift to you. Take joy in it and in Me."

I nearly cried as I held out my hands and let the snowflakes fall on my gloves. It didn't feel cold, though. It felt like God's hand was holding on tightly to mine. It felt as comforting and satisfying as a long embrace from the one you love the most. The joy was overwhelming, God's touch so warm and so near I couldn't help but laugh, releasing all my sorrow and welcoming this new season of joy.

I gingerly let my fingertips touch the side of the car as I crossed to the passenger side to take it for a test run. As soon as we sat in the car, as with Urnie, the name came to me at once. "Baby." I whispered, as if the name itself was, in fact, a breakthrough. To me, I guess it was.

Nolan gave me a funny look. "Baby?"

I nodded my head enthusiastically. "Nobody puts Baby in the corner." A quirked grin crept up the side of my face and broke into a full-blown smile.

He shook his head and shrugged at the *Dirty Dancing* reference, repeating the phrase in an exasperated, laughing tone, "Nobody puts Baby in the corner."

It was perfect. I thanked the man for holding the car for us, and he said, "Well, I know what my daughter would have said if I let a good deal like this slip away, and I didn't want your stepdad to have to deal with that." Laughter spilled forth from the merry little party, and I was full of gratitude.

We paid the owner; if it wasn't for the snow and God's unmistakable presence, I might have scarcely believed the car was finally mine. But it was snowing and God was certainly there and I knew with all my heart He had provided yet again, as He always would. We drove to a nearby Mexican restaurant for dinner. I don't know if it was simply the joy of the moment or if the restaurant was really that good, but the food was phenomenal. Joy has a way of making everything in the world seem brighter. I smiled as I ate my tacos and chips and salsa with queso, thanking God once again for providing abundantly.

On the way home, we stopped at a gas station to use the bathroom and fill up the tank. Inside, I noticed a brand of Nicaraguan coffee sitting on top of the coffee machine. All the sorrow and longing I felt for Nicaragua slammed into my chest, catching me completely off guard. The mask I had become used to wearing felt suffocating, and all my memories of what the pandemic had taken away from me surfaced. It wasn't that I had forgotten my pain for the foreign country—I thought about it every day. It was that I hadn't expected Satan to try and steal my joy again *so quickly*.

The rest of the way home, my joy seemed a bit dimmer. I prayed, and God reminded me of all the joy in my life; how the good would always outweigh the bad. With Him, He reminded me, my joy is unbreakable.

A couple days later, officially out of quarantine and officially legal to drive Baby with my spanking new Elvis license plate, I was free to ride the streets once again. It was so much fun visiting my friends after so long of being unable to hug them and be with them in person. But then I found out that my other grandmother, a healthcare worker, and toddler cousin contracted COVID. I wasn't quarantined, but I was worried for them.

A couple days later, despite my trying so hard to be careful, I accidentally scratched my car. My anxiety about making up finals (which I had missed because of quarantine) was overwhelming, even though I had confidence I would do well. Satan was trying to get at me, trying to break my joy and pull me away from God.

1 Peter 5:8 (NIV) reminds us to be prepared for Satan's attacks at all times. "Be alert and of sober mind. Your enemy the devil prowls around like a roaring lion looking for someone to devour." Even in the midst of great joy, Satan will try to attack you; we must always be prepared.

I chose to search for God in my trials, and while Satan attempted to overwhelm me, God sent joy to counter his advances. The good always outweighs the bad. We simply have to choose to see it, to find it. When I was in a dry spot with my writing, a letter came with the news that one of my poems was to be published in a poetry collection. I wasn't expecting the news at all, and I was so excited.

One morning as I was driving to school, exhausted from the workload and weary from not getting enough sleep, I rounded a curve in the road to see a full view of a radiant rose-gold sunrise beaming down on me. It gave me hope. I smiled, feeling God's presence fill the car as worship music played on the radio.

My best friend and I finally got to pick up the pair of fuzzy dice I had always fantasized about getting for my first car, Urnie, but never got around to. It was wonderful spending time together after nearly four weeks apart.

I send out messages with Bible verses once a week to encourage others and ask for prayer requests. My mom asked me to pray for her, which really touched my heart. I talked to God that very moment with the warmest feeling in my chest, thanking Him for this opportunity.

I prayed and prayed and put a lot of work into studying for finals, and I ended up with an A. All that worrying for nothing! I know I only passed because I chose to trust in God even if I failed. I chose to maintain my unbreakable joy whether I was victorious or temporarily defeated, because both success and failure would help me grow closer to God.

We have to choose joy no matter what we are facing. We must choose hope and love and patience if we want to see God at work in our lives. We have to choose to follow Him, not in spite of what we *may* face, but because of what we *will* face. He is the only One who can carry us through it all.

We must remember that the good always outweighs the bad, even if we have trouble seeing it. Ask God to reveal it to you. When I feel discouraged or tired, I simply remember Baby in the snow, God's gift for my obedience, and choose to hope no matter what's thrown my way. I know God has a plan, and His plan will bring greater joy than mine ever could.

Chemistry Teacher

A couple weeks before Christmas, my dad and stepmom tested positive for COVID-19, so I had to quarantine for fourteen days. I couldn't attend school in person, so I had to do all my work virtually. One day, this was how my chemistry teacher, Ms. Mullins, decided to take attendance:

Attendance Assignment

"This morning on the way to school, a song called "Truth Be Told" by Matthew West came on the radio, and the chorus really hit me. It said,
"'I'm fine, yeah I'm fine oh I'm fine. Hey, I'm fine,' but I'm not
I'm broken.
And when it's out of control I say, 'It's under control,' but it's not
I don't know why it's so hard to admit it
When being honest is the only way to fix it
There's no failure, no fall

There's no sin you don't already know
So let the truth be told."

This year will obviously stand out in history as the year of the pandemic, but many of us have pandemics of our own going on that no one knows about or understands—that have nothing to do with COVID. Well, some of them might, but most don't. So today, because I needed a way to take attendance, I decided to give you a chance to say something in confidence. I need you to respond so I know you are attending virtually. You don't have to share anything you don't want to share. You can just tell me you are present and hit submit. Or you can share something if you want. It is up to you. The only thing I ask is that you are honest. My greatest sadness over this semester is that I didn't get to spend the entire five months with you in person—I lost the chance to get to know you."

Most people probably only responded with "Present" or "Here," but I was touched by Ms. Mullins' love for her students. I chose to tell her something more. A week earlier, before I was quarantined, I told Ms. Mullins about the book I was writing while going over my grades for the quarter. I can't remember exactly how it came up in conversation, but we started talking about our favorite books and places to read; then, I told her how much I loved to write and that I was writing this book.

She was so excited and wanted to hear all about it. She even told me she looked forward to reading it one day.

Ms. Mullins has a faith that I admire. Don't get me wrong, she is an extremely challenging teacher, but the way she cares for her students is unlike any other teacher I've encountered.

She brought us little bags of candy for Halloween and Christmas and made sure to offer some before every test because it helps us focus. Sometimes she even gave us snacks after completing a lab. She was patient when we didn't understand and kind when we were upset. She encouraged us to do our best and helped us when she knew we weren't performing at our full potential. She affirmed that we could do anything we set our minds to. She listened to us. She prayed for us.

For this reason, I decided to respond to the attendance assignment with something true, just like she asked. I didn't care if nobody else responded with something heartfelt: I just wanted Ms. Mullins to know how much I appreciate her. And what better way to show her than by writing something thoughtful?

Dear Ms. Mullins,

Thank you so much for sharing this song. It is beautiful and definitely something I needed to hear today. I know I told you a little about the book I was writing a couple weeks ago, but I want to share what inspired it.

Quarantine was a time of much darkness, and because of this, a time of great joy. Sorrow and joy go hand in hand; one cannot exist without the other. Throughout the long months of social distancing and sickness, God taught me a lot about hope and patience and stillness. It was hard at first, but now I see quarantine as a blessing. The inspiration for my book came from quarantine, and this book has been one of the greatest blessings of my life thus far. Please pray that it will encourage many people in the future. It's called *Everlasting Light*; it's about choosing hope and joy in times of darkness. I am who I am, not in spite of my struggles, but because of them. The way we choose to view our lives changes the way we live.

Ms. Mullins, I hope you choose to live by God's everlasting light, the only light that never fades, for the rest of your days. It's the only thing that will get you through the trials of life.

In other news, my dad tested positive for COVID, so I will be in quarantine for the next couple of weeks. Please pray that he would heal and use this time to refocus and strengthen his relationship with God.

Please pray for me to continue viewing quarantine as a blessing even though I'm disappointed that there are so many things I'll miss out on this holiday season. I know there is good in every situation, and I have confidence God will provide more inspiration for my writing over the next two weeks. I choose joy, and I pray you will, too.

Much love, Lily K. Lewis

Later, she emailed me about my attendance response:
"Lily,

I so appreciated you taking the time to write your note this morning, and I appreciate your insights. I, too, believe God is the only way we can survive anything. He has been my light since I was twelve years old. I have survived much worse than this pandemic/quarantine, and He has walked me through it all. It was only by His grace and mercy that I made it. I have a powerful testimony of His faithfulness. Maybe someday we will be able to meet face-to-face (without masks) and share our stories. Please know that I will be praying for your family during this time of quarantine—for health, but also for peace and a time to be still. If you need anything, please let me know.

I know I will have you in class again in upcoming years. I am so looking forward to it. And yes—I choose joy because of the One who lives in my heart. Thank you for making my day (and my semester)!"

Again, I emailed her back:
Ms. Mullins,

Thank you for sharing these kind words with me! I hope we get to share our stories one day as well. Thank you so much for all the prayers.

I am so glad you chose joy, and I pray you will always remember God in dark times.

Chemistry has been my favorite class this semester, and I look forward to having you again in the future! Thanks for being an awesome teacher.

This was her final response:

"Lily,

Thank you for always being an amazing student and for always being a light!"

It was this last email that touched me more than anything. For so long, one of my constant prayers has been to be a light and encourage others. Ms. Mullins couldn't have possibly known that was my prayer if I hadn't told her, and I never mentioned it. The fact that she sees me as a light warms my heart. It was God reminding me my labor is not in vain, that I *am* making a difference. One person at a time.

To live a life of everlasting light, we have to take every opportunity to encourage others that is presented to us. It doesn't matter what others say or think or do—it matters what you decide to do. Will you take action or watch opportunities as they slip away?

Ephesians 5:16 (ESV) instructs us to "make the most of every opportunity, because the days are evil."

We have a short amount of time here on earth, so we should make the most of the time we have. Whatever we may be facing now is nothing compared to the glory of eternity if we are faithful.

Maybe as a parent you're struggling to be patient with your kids. Remember you only have a short time to be with them while they are young. Take a deep breath and pray. Choose to take every opportunity to show them what God's love looks like by being kind, patient, and generous.

Maybe you're a teenager who forgets to appreciate all your parents do for you. Take the opportunity to show them how much you love them by completing your chores, watching your tone (as my parents always say), and just spending time with them. Showing appreciation doesn't have to be grand. It just has to be *genuine*.

Whether you're reaching out to a teacher, friend, or loved one, take every opportunity to share God's message. And when someone shares it with you, don't ignore them. Wherever you are or whatever you may be doing, don't pass up the opportunity to be a light. Opportunities, as much as blessings and delivered promises, are a gift from God. Don't let them slip through your fingers. Make the right choice and hold on tightly.

Chosen

At the end of my sophomore year, I went to a graduation party for one of my good friends; it didn't go at all as I expected. Grabbing some food and sitting down to enjoy it, everyone talked and hung out for a little while, catching up and saying heartfelt goodbyes. Jah'Karious, a guy on my Academic Decathlon team, sat at my table. After a little while, I noticed that he was very quiet, looking pensive and solemn. I asked him what he was thinking about; a beautiful conversation about Matthew 9:27-31 ensued. It is one I will never forget. This chapter is inspired by that conversation, and I want to encourage you, Jah'Karious, to keep preaching. You have a bright future ahead of you!

Matthew 9:27-31 (NKJV) says this, "When Jesus departed from there, two blind men followed Him, crying out and saying, 'Son of David, have mercy on us!' And when He had come into the house, the blind men came to Him. And Jesus said to them, 'Do you believe that I am able to do this?' They said to Him, 'Yes, Lord.' Then He touched their eyes, saying

'According to your faith let it be to you.' And their eyes were opened. And Jesus sternly warned them, saying, 'See that no one knows it.' But when they had departed, they spread the news about Him in all that country."

The first thing that sticks out to me about this story, oddly enough, is the ending. Jesus instructed the healed men to keep quiet about the miracle He performed. They immediately disobeyed Jesus and told anyone who would listen in *the whole country*. Although the two men should have listened to Jesus's instructions, I completely understand where they are coming from. If a man claiming to be the Savior of the world healed my vision, I would want everyone else to know about it. At first, I wondered why Jesus would tell the men this. Didn't Jesus want other people to hear about Him? And then it hit me. That was exactly it: Jesus wanted people to hear about *Him*, not the things He did.

This realization came full circle at a short weekend retreat during the fall of the school year. The speaker was talking about a different story, but the concept was similar. The purpose of healing and miracles and wonders is to confirm and strengthen the message that Jesus is alive and God is real. However, it's the *message* that connects us all—the Good News of salvation, love, and hope—that Jesus came to share.

Through the sacrificial love of Jesus, we have been saved, and because we have been saved, we have the hope of heaven in our hearts. This hope is like a thread that ties us all together. It connects believer to believer in a beautiful web of light and joy with Jesus, who tied the first knots at the center of it all.

From the story in Matthew, we know that the two blind men believed in Jesus. It's this belief that healed them. However, I want to take this a step deeper. There are some other things about this story that stick out to me.

How did the blind men find Jesus? In the passage, it doesn't say anybody led them. If no one guided them to Jesus, how could they have found Him? Here's where the thread connecting all believers comes back into play: the men believed. If these men believed, that means they were connected to Jesus through hope and light. Light…

The thread that connected them could have led them toward Jesus, yes, but there's also another possibility I would like to consider. The blind men lived in total darkness. They couldn't see anything. Jesus is often described as light; where light is there can be no darkness. This is a fact. So, if these men were living in darkness and came across Jesus (who is Light), there couldn't have been any darkness anymore. I think it was Jesus's light that led the men to Him, a path of joy and hope cutting through darkness and sorrow.

This leads back to where we started. After these men had found the Light, they went and shared with everybody what Jesus *did*. *This* was their biggest mistake.

We have to learn from Scripture and apply it to our lives. God chose and led these men to Jesus so we could read this story in future generations, learn from it, and avoid making the same mistakes. I believe all stories in the Bible are designed for our growth even now. There is something we can learn from every verse. So, what does this teach us?

We were chosen to believe and share our faith with others. But, when we are sharing the Good News with others, we have to share about Jesus Himself, not just what He can do for us. To live a life of everlasting light, we must follow the Light until there's no more darkness and tie a knot around our heart, linking it to Jesus. We must believe. We must hope. We must love. We must choose because we were chosen.

Perpetual Beauty

Everyone struggles with body image. No matter how confident others seem, they have doubts and insecurities, too. Many people allow these insecurities to consume them. I was one of those people only a few years ago.

I was really insecure about my body and struggled to find beauty within myself. But after a fall retreat, I realized I needed to stop focusing on my outward appearance and start focusing on my inward appearance.

The first thing I did when I got home was grab a pair of scissors, a roll of tape, different colored markers, some notebook paper, and my Bible. I opened up its pages and read all the verses, all of God's promises and reassurances, about true beauty and about who God says I am. I wrote the words on notebook paper, cut them out, and taped them to my bathroom mirror, all the while reflecting on how God made me a beautifully crafted vessel for His purpose and light to shine through into the lives of others.

"Come now, let us reason together, says the Lord." Isaiah 1:18 (ESV) continues, "Though your sins are like scarlet, they shall be as white as snow; though they are red like crimson, they shall become like wool."

I am forgiven. Thank You, Jesus, for Your sacrifice. Because of You, I can start anew.

"I have been crucified with Christ. It is no longer I who live," reads a worship song taken straight from Scripture, "but Christ who lives in me. And the life that I now live in the flesh I live by the faith of the Son of God, who loved me and gave himself for me." (Galatians 2:20 ESV)

I am crucified with Christ. I no longer live for myself. I live to follow Him. I am dead to my selfishness and envy and anger. I am alive to all things good and holy. I am alive to Christ. It is Him who lives, not me. I am crucified with Christ.

1 Corinthians 10:13 (ESV) maintains, "No temptation has overtaken you that is not common to man. God is faithful, and he will not let you be tempted beyond your ability, but with the temptation he will also provide the way of escape, that you may be able to endure it."

I am tempted, but *I am capable* of overcoming my sin when I draw from the power of our good, faithful, reliable God, our everlasting source of strength.

Romans 3:23-25 (ESV) reminds me of God's sympathetic heart towards us. "For all have sinned and fall short of the glory of God, and are justified by his grace as a gift, through the redemption that is in Christ Jesus, whom God put forward as a propitiation by his blood, to be received by faith. This was to show God's righteousness, because in his divine forbearance he had passed over former sins."

I am a sinner, and I am saved by grace. *I am understood.*

2 Corinthians 4:16 (ESV) describes why we should never give up. "So, we do not lose heart. Though our outer self is wasting away, our inner self is being renewed day by day."

Day by day, *I am renewed.*

2 Corinthians 5:17 (ESV) says, "If anyone is in Christ, he is a new creation. The old has passed away; behold, the new has come."

I am not defined by my past. I am defined by who I am becoming; I am defined by who God made me to be. Since I have been baptized, *I am a new creation.*

1 Corinthians 6:18-20 (ESV) commands, "Flee from sexual immorality. Every other sin a person commits is outside the body, but the sexually immoral person sins against his own body. Or do you not know that your body is a temple of the Holy Spirit within you, whom you have from God? You are not your own, for you were bought with a price. So, glorify God in your body."

I was bought at a price, made to glorify God through my body. *I am a temple of the Lord, and I am not my own.*

Acts 2:38 (ESV) says this, "And Peter said to them, 'Repent and be baptized every one of you in the name of Christ Jesus for the forgiveness of your sins, and you will receive the gift of the Holy Spirit.'"

I am spirit-filled.

I prayed Psalm 51:10 (ESV), a song of David, which pleads, "Create in me a clean, O God, and renew a right spirit within me."

I am made pure. I am made innocent. I am made holy through confession and God's answered prayers of forgiveness.

"Have I not commanded you?" questions Joshua 1:9 (ESV), "Be strong and courageous. Do not be frightened, and do not be dismayed, for the Lord your God is with you wherever you go."

I am not afraid.

Ephesians 6:12 (ESV) reminds us who the enemy is. "For we do not wrestle against flesh and blood, but against the rulers, against the authorities, against cosmic powers over this present darkness, against the spiritual forces of evil in the heavenly places."

I am wrestling with the evil of this world for the glory of God. *I am fighting for God, with God*, taking a stand against Satan. God gives me the strength and the will and the way.

Ruth 1:12,14-18 (ESV) tells the story of a daughter-in-law who refused to leave the side of her husband's mother after the death of all the men in their immediate family. "'Turn back, my daughters; go your way, for I am too old to have a husband…' Then they lifted up their voices and wept again. And Orpah kissed her mother-in-law, but Ruth clung to her. And she said, 'See, your sister-in-law has gone back to her people and to her gods; return after your sister-in-law.' But Ruth said, 'Do not urge me to leave you or to return from following you. For where you go I will go, and where you lodge I will lodge. Your people shall be my people, and your God my God. Where you die I will die, and there will I be buried. May the Lord do so to me and more also if anything but death parts me from you.' And when Naomi saw that she was determined to go with her, she said no more."

I will never stop trying, never give up on anyone, not even myself. *I am determined*, and so I will make it through whatever I am facing, helping others along the way, and we will make it through stronger.

Romans 8:28 (ESV) assures us, "And we know that for those who love God all things work together for good, for those who are called according to His purpose."

I am certain. Certain that I love God, certain that all things will work for good, and certain that God has a plan. *I am called,* and I'm certain I'm called *according to His purpose.*

Romans 5:8 (ESV) tenderly reminds us, "But God shows his love for us in that while we were still sinners, Christ died for us."

Jesus was willing to die so I could have life, so we could have true life, the ultimate expression of love. Because of this selfless act, *I am worthy.*

Genesis 1:27-28 (NIV) says, "So God created man in His own image; in the image of God He created him; male and female He created them. Then God blessed them…"

I am enough—we are all more than enough. We were created in the likeness of God, who exceeds all expectations and who has no limits. We were made in the image of the all-powerful Creator of the universe, the Lord of Lords, the King of Kings. *We were created to be more than enough. We were created to be God's people.*

Proverbs 1:7 (ESV) says, "The fear of the Lord is the beginning of knowledge; fools despise wisdom and instruction."

James 1:5 (NKJV) promises, "If any of you lacks wisdom, let him ask of God, who gives to all liberally and without reproach, and it will be given to him."

I am wise because I prayed for wisdom and God provided. I chose joy and hope and love. Only through Christ can there be wisdom, only through the fear of the Lord can knowledge be found. *I am wise because I follow God and His commandments.*

Philippians 4:13 (NKJV) says it this way, "I can do all things through Christ who strengths me."

Luke 1:37 (NKJV) builds upon this, imploring us to take action because "… with God nothing will be impossible."

I am empowered through Christ to use my talents and blessings to bring God glory. I will always say yes to God, not in spite of my fears and doubts, but because I know He will overcome them.

1 Peter 2:9 (ESV) declares, "But you are a chosen race, a royal priesthood, a holy nation, a people for his own possession, that you may proclaim the excellencies of him who called you out of darkness and into his marvelous light."

I am chosen. Chosen to share the Good News, chosen to follow Jesus, chosen to be called a child of God. *I am chosen to live in God's everlasting light.*

Psalm 43:5 (MSG) says these words, "Why are you down in the dumps, dear soul? Why are you crying the blues? Fix my eyes on God— soon I'll be praising again. He puts a smile on my face. He's my God."

Even when my soul is downcast, focusing on God puts a smile on my face. *I am hopeful* because I believe God answers prayers. *I am hopeful* because God provides abundantly. I need only wait patiently.

Daniel 3:17-18 (ESV) asserts, "If this be so, our God whom we serve is able to deliver us from the burning fiery furnace, and he will deliver us out of your hand, O king. But if not, be it known to you, O king, that we will not serve your gods or worship the golden image that you have set up."

I will trust God no matter what and serve Him alone.

Paul writes in Romans 15:13 (ESV), "May the God of hope fill you with all joy and peace in believing, so that by the power of the Holy Spirit you may abound in hope."

I am joyful because I have hope in the Lord in all circumstances, whatever may build me up or befall me.

"And whatever you do in word or deed," Colossians 3:17 (ESV) encourages us, "do everything in the name of the Lord Jesus, giving thanks to the Father through him."

I am thankful. I choose to live every moment in gratitude to the Lord by serving Him through my actions.

Psalm 23 (ESV) never ceases to soothe my soul and longing for peace or adventure during sufferings and quiet times. "The Lord is my shepherd; I shall not want. He makes me to lie down in green pastures; He leads me beside the still waters. He restores my soul; He leads me in the paths of righteousness for His name's sake. Yea, though I walk through the valley of the shadow of death, I will fear no evil; For You are with me; Your rod and your staff, they comfort me. You prepare a table before me in the presence of my enemies, You anoint my head with oil; My cup runs over. Surely goodness and mercy shall follow me all the days of my life and I will dwell in the house of the Lord forever."

I am content. God is always with me. He is all I need.

Galatians 5:1 (ESV) proclaims, "Christ has set us free; stand firm therefore, and do not submit again to a yoke of slavery."

I am free, and I will not be taken captive by sins and Satan's lies again.

Luke 15:11- 32 tells the story of the prodigal son and the father who welcomed him home with open arms. After spending all his inheritance on wild parties, prostitutes, and other unfulfilling things, the son came to his senses. He was starving, weak, and lost. Choosing to return home and suffer humiliation rather than die, he prepared to beg his father for a place as a servant in his house.

Luke 15:20-24 (NKJV) says, "And he arose and came to his father. But when he was still a great way off, his father saw him and had compassion, and ran and fell on his neck and kissed him. And the son said to him, 'Father, I have sinned against heaven and in your sight, and I am no longer worthy to be called your son.' But the father said to his servants, 'Bring out the best robe and put it on him and put a ring on his hand and sandals on his feet. And bring the fattened calf here and kill it and let us eat and be merry; for this my son was dead and is alive again; he was lost and is found.' And they began to be merry."

When I was lost, God ran towards me and pulled me from my place of hopelessness. I was falling, but I landed in God's embrace. *I am found.*

Galatians 5:13 (ESV) teaches us, "For you were called to freedom, brothers. Only do not use your freedom as an opportunity for the flesh, but through love serve one another."

I am made to be a humble servant, just as Jesus taught us to be.

"And no creature is hidden from his sight," Hebrews 4:13 (ESV) goes on to say, "but all are naked and exposed to the eyes of him to whom we must give account."

I am fully known by God and loved not in spite of my mistakes and flaws, but because of them and because God's love is made perfect in its immortality compared to the conditional, temporary love of the world.

In John 10:10 (NCV), Jesus says, "…I came to give life—life in all its fullness."

I am alive, living life to the fullest joy and hope and purpose possible, because *I am following Christ.*

In Psalm 46:10 (NVC), God calmingly whispers, "…Be still and know that I am God. I will be praised in all the nations; I will be praised throughout the earth."

In Proverbs 3:24 (ESV), the Lord softly whispers, "If you lie down, you will not be afraid; when you lie down, your sleep will be sweet."

I am still and quiet. I rest in peace because God's soft touch, His tender whisper, speaks to my heart and comforts me.

James 2:17 (ESV) cautions us to be active in our walk with Christ. "So faith by itself, if it does not have works, is dead."

I am active in my faith. My faith is alive and well.

Ecclesiastes 3:11 (ESV) says, "He has made everything beautiful in its time. Also, he has put eternity into man's heart, yet so that he cannot find out what God has done from the beginning even to the end."

I am focused on God. I have my eyes set on heaven and my heart set on God's love as the goal, purpose, and drive of my life.

Psalm 139:14 (NKJV) paints a picture of how God created us and why we should praise Him. "I will praise You, for I am fearfully and wonderfully made; Marvelous are your works, and that my soul knows very well."

I am fearfully and wonderfully made. I know it and believe it with all I am and all I am becoming.

"The Lord is my strength and my song, and he has become my salvation; this is my God, and I will praise him, my father's God, and I exalt him," sang Moses and the people of Israel in Exodus 15:2 (ESV).

I am strong because the Lord is my strength.

John 3:16 (NKJV) reveals the depth of God's love for us: "For God so loved the world that He gave His only begotten Son, that whoever believes in Him should not perish but have everlasting life."

I am loved. I am loved enough that Jesus died on the cross so I could experience everlasting light in my life.

"Do not let your adornment be merely outward—arranging the hair, wearing gold, or putting on fine apparel—," 1 Peter 3:3-4 (NKJV) instructs us, "rather let it be the hidden person of the heart, with the incorruptible beauty of a gentle and quiet spirit, which is very precious in the sight of God."

I am beautiful and precious to our gentle God.

Proverbs 3:26 (ESV) repeats to us what God has been trying to instill in us our whole lives: "For the Lord will be your confidence and will keep your foot from being caught."

I am confident because the Lord is guiding my steps. I believe in His Word and His promises. With all my heart, all my soul, and all my strength, *I believe.*

Now that I believe all these things, Matthew 5:14-16 (NKJV) shines in my life. "You are the light of the world. A city that is set on a hill cannot be hidden. Nor do they light a lamp and put it under a basket, but on a lampstand, and it gives light to all who are in the house. Let your light so shine before men, that they may see your good works and glorify your Father in heaven."

I am a light. I am God's light.

And when I was finished taping the words on the mirror, I looked myself in the eye and prayed. "God, please help me to see myself the way You see me. I was stubborn, cold, afraid, lost in sin… The world told me I was ugly, hated, never enough, and unwanted. But God, now I know the truth. With You, I am loved. I am beautiful. I am worthy. I am more than enough. I am alive. And I am found. Thank You for bringing me to this place of confidence and light. Thank You for teaching me to believe in Your promises. I pray that others might find this peace in belief, too. Truly, I praise You. Amen." And then, I smiled. You will never forget the first time you look in the mirror and smile because you like what you see.

This was my prayer every day, every time I looked in the mirror. Eventually, I became confident in who I was and how I looked, but most importantly I learned to recognize God in myself and others. Before long, I didn't need to see the words on my mirror every day to remember and believe in them anymore. For almost my entire life, I allowed the world to dominate my opinion of myself. The world seemed to tell me that I would never be enough. But God whispered to me that I am beautiful, loved, and worthy. He whispered the truth to me until I believed it with all my heart. Believing in perpetual beauty through Christ is what gives us confidence in ourselves, inside and out.

The day I took the words down and taped them into my journal, so I could always look back in case I needed a reminder of God's promises, was a joyous occasion. I could feel God smiling with me, proud of me for overcoming my insecurities and learning that true, perpetual beauty is about finding God in yourself and believing His promises.

When we believe in God's truth, God can use us to be a light to others like never before, shining His everlasting light through our love and respect for ourselves and others. You don't have to be perfect to be a light. You just have to know how to find God in yourself, so you can see Him in others.

Live in the Light

Before 2019, I don't ever remember seeing a beautiful sunset during the winter months. I'm certain there were many, but all I know is that my world felt too dark to see it. My eyes were blinded by the dreariness of freezing weather and numb extremities. My heart was cold because of all I had been through.

On my fourteenth birthday, I don't remember why exactly, but it was not a good day. After school, all I wanted was for there to be a beautiful sunset, colorful enough to inspire the smile that eluded me. But there was only gray and nothing but clouds. My heart fell and I became discouraged.

I don't remember catching any lively sunsets that winter. All I remember seeing: gray. All I remember feeling: cold.

During the summer between my fourteenth and fifteenth birthdays, something changed while I was at camp. Suddenly, my eyes were opened, and I could feel God more clearly. I could hear Him and see Him; I wanted to live for Him. My heart was thawed.

That year and the year after, the sunsets were gorgeous on my birthday, bringing a smile to my face. But when I look back on my fourteenth birthday with gray skies, I can't help but thank God.

In the same way I chose to praise God when the stars weren't out, God used the cloudy birthday to teach me to live in the light even when the sun isn't shining.

On my fourteenth birthday, I didn't have the right response to the gray skies, because I allowed myself to become discouraged. But when my heart and eyes were opened before my next birthday, and because I chose to praise God no matter what happened, He sent a vibrant sunset.

1 John 1:5-7 (NCV) says this, "Here is the message we have heard from Christ and now announce to you: God is light, and in him there is no darkness at all. So, if we say we have fellowship with God, but we continue living in the darkness, we are liars and do not follow the truth. But if we live in the light, as God is in the light, we can share fellowship with each other. Then the blood of Jesus, God's Son, cleanses us from every sin."

When fighting through trials, we have to choose to walk in the light if we want God to hear us and answer our prayers. We have to choose to walk in the light, being baptized and remaining faithful, if we want to be forgiven. Living in the light is about recognizing hope and beauty shining through the darkness and choosing to trust God before we even know what we will face.

If we know God and yet do not trust Him or follow His commands, we are walking in the darkness. Satan wants us to live in the darkness; he does everything he can to drag us into sin and trouble and lies. He tries his best to blind us to the light and draw us away from God.

But when we choose to live in the light, truly choose to allow nothing to stop us from seeing His goodness, Satan will bolt. Satan is a coward. If we stand our ground, he will run away. James 4:7 (NIV) assures us of this, "Submit yourselves, then, to God. Resist the devil, and he will flee from you."

Submitting to God is required for living in the light. James 4:10 (NIV) continues, "Humble yourselves before the Lord, and he will lift you up."

Living in the light is about being humble, putting away our pride, surrendering to God, and trusting His light to shine the way through our darkest moments.

On Christmas Eve in 2020, the sunset was so wonderful that I couldn't resist going for a run. I would have taken a walk, but it was about twenty-eight to thirty degrees outside. I figured the faster I ran, the quicker I would warm up.

I grinned as I ran, even though my nose was running, and my chest was heavy in the cold air. This is the first sunset I can remember vividly lowering toward the horizon on Christmas Eve. The colors spread across the sky in streaks of pink and gold, orange and a hint of purple.

This holiday season had definitely not been ideal, with three of my parents, my grandmother and aunt, and a couple of my friends sick with COVID. We couldn't get together to open presents or bake cookies. We couldn't hug each other or celebrate as a family. Those who were quarantined were stuck at home; those who were sick were bedridden.

But as I ran, I remembered the birthday of gray skies and thanked God for shining this marvelous sunset into a dark season of my life. It was just what I needed to lift my Christmas spirit. Soon enough everyone was well, and we were able to celebrate as a family. Because I trusted God, He provided healing and beauty and inspiration abundantly. Because I trusted God, He carried me through those trials and into fellowship with my family and friends once again. Because I trust God, He helps me to live in the light.

Choosing to live a life of everlasting light rather than a life of eternal darkness takes a humble heart and an open mind. Deciding to live in the light doesn't mean your days will always be sunny. It means that even when the world around you is dark, you still determine to walk in the path of God's light, the light of fellowship and hope and joy that never fades. Living in the light is a choice you have to make for yourself. God's light always shines: we only have to choose to see it.

Singing in the Car

My dad and I have always been really close. One of the places we bonded over the most was in the car. When he picked me up after school, took me to get milkshakes after church some Wednesday nights, or drove me to see the latest Disney movie in theaters, we would always talk and laugh together. We talked about all we were going through, how our days were, our hopes for the future. I shared the stories I cooked up in my head during recess or the books I was currently reading, and he shared funny stories from his job and new songs he'd found.

We would also have deep spiritual conversations. He would laugh when I asked questions that required a lot of thought during the early morning car rides to school or when I surprised him with a clever insight. We talked about our favorite verses, what we had learned in church, and our opinions on various topics. We would occasionally even debate.

But more than the milkshakes and laughs and movies, I loved it when my dad and I would sing in the car. My dad has a rich, deep voice; he's a wonderful singer, too. Strangers will randomly ask if he's a radio show host or a sports commentator. I'm dead serious. People who hear him singing compliment his voice. When he preaches, he sometimes likes to get a little loud to make the people who aren't paying attention jump. It's hilarious.

When we sang in the car, my dad singing bass, me swapping between soprano and alto depending on my mood, we didn't sing just any songs. Sure, we would listen to different soundtracks and sing along, but most often, we would sing praise to God.

The chorus of one of our favorite songs, "Just a Little Talk with Jesus" by Cleavant Derricks, goes like this:

> "Now let us have a little talk with Jesus
> Let us tell Him all about our troubles
> He will hear our faintest cry
> And He will answer by and by
> Now when you feel a little pray'r wheel turning
> And you know a little fire is burning
> You will find a little talk with Jesus
> Makes it right."

If there is anything my dad taught me, it's that a little talk with Jesus really does make it right. When I had a bad day or made a mistake, he would remind me of God's goodness by singing with me in the car. He was always encouraging, and no matter where he was, he was always singing praise to God.

Another of our songs, "A Beautiful Life" by William M. Golden, says this,

> "Each day I'll do a golden deed,
> By helping those who are in need;
> My life on earth is but a span,
> And so I'll do the best I can.

Life's evening sun is sinking low,
A few more days, and I must go
To meet the deeds that I have done,
Where there will be no setting sun."

True life is spent constantly praising God, even in the most unlikely places. True life is about viewing our experiences through a heavenly lens and choosing to discover what God intended for us to learn. True life is about the connections we form with people by worshipping God together, because that's when everlasting light comes into the picture.

Part Four:

Break My Heart

Break My Heart

by Clint Rhodes

Break my heart, dear Lord,
Tear the barriers down.
Show me in convicting tears
the glory of Your crown.
My heart is hard, my soul so weak,
the ways of evil cut so deep.
I need You, Lord, to come inside
and gently break my heart.

Purpose of Pain

G od doesn't waste pain.

In 2018, I got the flu. I was thirteen years old. It's the worst sickness I have ever experienced. I couldn't get out of bed for weeks. I was either burning hot or freezing cold with no in-between; I threw up a lot and didn't eat very much. Walking, even to the bathroom a few feet from my bed, was difficult. My body was so weak that my legs would shake, and I would have to lean against something for support. I grew paler than I had ever been before and being a redhead, I'm already *really* pale. I was coughing uncontrollably, sneezing, and my nose wouldn't stop running. My head pounded and my body ached, and I felt like I couldn't breathe. I was miserable.

When I thought it couldn't get any worse, my fever reached one hundred and four degrees, and my mom drove me to the emergency room. There the doctor told me that I had contracted pneumonia.

I was stuck in bed for weeks after that. The days dragged by in a haze of restless sleep and confusion. I couldn't focus on anything but the sickness. I couldn't read because my head hurt so bad; I couldn't go for a walk to get some fresh air—I could barely even sit up.

For those of you that don't know, the basic definition of pneumonia is a lung inflammation caused by bacteria or a viral infection, in which the air sacs fill with mucus and pus and other great stuff like that. This infection can be life-threatening, especially to children and elderly people. My symptoms included cough with phlegm or pus, fever, chills, and difficulty breathing. It felt as if there was a weight on my chest. I didn't have much of an appetite, and I was constantly sweating, shivering, or both. Even though all I was doing was lying in bed, my heart seemed to beat double-time.

On top of all this, the medicine I was given for the flu had some serious side effects. Aside from the physical side effects, the medicine had a severe impact on my mental health. I was in a depressive mood, unable to muster up the energy to do anything; I was stuck in a state of confusion.

Healing was a slow process. When it was time to go back to school, I was better, but I could still feel the weight on my chest from when I was sick. The fact that I was at an entirely new school didn't help my anxiety. Every time I would get stressed or worried, I could feel the weight on my chest, constantly pressing down on me. My heart would beat faster, and I would get short of breath.

I vaguely remember praying while I was sick, but I know my heart wasn't in it. I believed in God; I had even been baptized a few years before, but I didn't trust in God like I should have. Instead, I got caught up in the sickness and fear and worry. I allowed it to consume my mind, just like Satan wanted. The whole time, God was there calling to me, begging me to cry out to Him, to seek Him with all my heart. But I couldn't hear Him. My eyes were blinded by all that I was facing. My heart was closed to Him.

Soccer season came a couple months after I was sick. I couldn't run like I used to. My body was still so exhausted. My mental health and spiritual life were not yet where they needed to be.

Summer came a couple months after that. It was time to go to camp, my favorite part of the year. Every year, camp encouraged me to keep fighting, to keep seeking God. But this year, some girls were mean to me and my friends, and camp just wasn't as fun.

The rest of the year flew by as I started eighth grade. I was mostly healthy except for seasonal allergies and the stomach bug. Right before I was about to attend a weekend youth rally in Gatlinburg in the February of 2019, I knew something was wrong. My skin was clammy, my heart started beating faster, and I felt sick to my stomach. The weight on my chest was back with a vengeance, only this time it was more anxiety than sickness.

I went to the doctor… And I tested positive for the flu again.

I couldn't stop the tears that slipped down my face. I was so scared. I didn't want to get sick again, not like last time. I didn't understand why God would do this. When I got home, I prayed. And this time, I meant it.

They didn't give me the same medicine as the previous year. They had a new treatment that simply consisted of two pills. Relieved that I wouldn't have to take the same medicine as last year, but still wary of the new medicine, I swallowed the pills tentatively.

Despite all my fears, my symptoms were not nearly as bad as the last time. Within a few days, my fever was gone, and I was well. I marveled at how quickly I was healed. I was even able to go on the trip.

I thanked God like I never had before. It seemed impossible that I could heal so fast, feel strong so soon after. I began to trust God more and more.

Months passed, and then it was time for camp again. Filled with memories of the mean girls from the previous year, I was a little nervous but eager to learn about Jesus and have fun with some of my closest friends.

I left this week of camp forever changed. Sun stained my skin once again and I was no longer deathly pale. Freckles splattered across my nose. I learned how to laugh again. I learned how to love like Jesus. Under the midnight stars, I realized that I wanted to be a writer and a missionary. I realized where I needed to work on my spiritual life and took action. There were so many brilliant friends and speakers who helped me find who I was and who I wanted to become. They inspired me to work towards my dreams. They inspired me to hope. They inspired me to be a light.

I left that week as a completely new person. I can scarcely recognize the girl I was before. I was sorrowful and dark and hurting. My joy was based on my circumstances. My heart was not in the right place.

God opened my eyes that week. I opened my heart to Him, and as He promised, He filled me with His everlasting light. It was like nothing I had ever experienced before. I became joyful and determined and whole. Jesus took the broken pieces of my life and rearranged them into a new masterpiece, with God at the center of everything. From that point on, I have served God faithfully. That doesn't mean I haven't messed up. It means I've made mistakes and come back stronger.

God uses the pain in our lives to prepare us for His plan. Sometimes our hearts have to break before they can open to God and whatever His will for our lives may be.

If I hadn't gotten the flu twice, I might never have turned to God like I did. I might not be who I am now. I might not have experienced the joy of His healing or the feeling of hope warming my heart. *God allows our hearts to break so He can heal us, teach us, and build us up stronger than ever before.*

I might not have realized I want to be a writer and a missionary. I might still be angry, lost, and confused. My joy might have remained conditional. If I hadn't gotten the flu twice, I might not be who I am today. And the thought of who I could have been, someone who doesn't live their life as a light, brings me more pain than sickness ever could.

For this reason, and so many others, I am so thankful that I was sick. God used my pain to prepare me to write. He used my pain to teach me how amazing He is, greater than anything I may be facing.

This sickness is what set everything in motion, the domino that knocked over the whole row. Without it, I probably would never have written this book. God took my life half-lived for Him, broke it, and mended it into a life fully lived to follow Him.

To live a life of everlasting light, we must allow our trials to open our eyes to God instead of closing our hearts to Him. Instead of questioning God when we face difficult situations, we should thank Him for the opportunity to grow closer to Him. He will provide. God will use your pain to bring light into your life and the lives of others when you choose to share what God has done for you. It may be difficult, but we have to share our stories about what God has done for us.

The purpose of pain isn't only to lead us towards God. It's a tool God has gifted us to bring others to Him as well. If we refuse to share our stories, we miss the opportunity to shine God's light on all those we encounter. It may hurt at first, but as you share your testimony the burden will lessen. Each time I share my story, the weight on my chest becomes lighter.

God won't waste your pain. Use it to bring glory to His kingdom.

Purpose of Fear

After contracting the flu the first time, I was scared to get sick again. I was afraid the weight on my chest would return heavier than ever before. I was afraid of missing out on things. I was afraid of being isolated, away from my friends and family again. I was afraid of being unable to care for myself and having to depend on others. I was afraid of being confined to my bed again, confused and depressed.

The second time I got the flu, I was afraid all my fears would become reality. My joy was so great when I was healed quickly—my relief was overwhelming. The purpose of fear is for God to show us that there was never really anything to be afraid of in the first place. Nothing is impossible for God; there is nothing He will not or cannot carry us through.

When we are lost, God provides the way back home. When we are hurting, He comforts us. When we are grappling with a difficult decision, He gives us wisdom. When we are afraid, He reminds us that there is nothing to be afraid of.

David, in an exuberant declaration of faith in Psalm 27:1-14 (NKJV), exclaimed,

"The LORD *is* my light and my salvation;
Whom shall I fear?
The LORD *is* the strength of my life;
Of whom shall I be afraid?
When the wicked came against me
To eat up my flesh,
My enemies and foes,
They stumbled and fell.
Though an army may encamp against me,
My heart shall not fear;
Though war may rise against me,
In this I *will be* confident.
One *thing* I have desired of the LORD,
That will I seek:
That I may dwell in the house of the LORD
All the days of my life,
To behold the beauty of the LORD,
And to inquire in His temple.
For in the time of trouble
He shall hide me in His pavilion;
In the secret place of His tabernacle
He shall hide me;
He shall set me high upon a rock.
And now my head shall be lifted up above my enemies all around me;
Therefore I will offer sacrifices of joy in His tabernacle;
I will sing, yes, I will sing praises to the LORD.
Hear, O LORD, *when* I cry with my voice!
Have mercy also upon me, and answer me.
When You said, "Seek My face,"

My heart said to You, "Your face, Lord, I will seek."

Do not hide Your face from me;

Do not turn Your servant away in anger;

You have been my help;

Do not leave me nor forsake me,

O God of my salvation.

When my father and my mother forsake me,

Then the Lord will take care of me.

Teach me Your way, O Lord,

And lead me in a smooth path, because of my enemies.

Do not deliver me to the will of my adversaries;

For false witnesses have risen against me,

And such as breathe out violence.

I would have lost heart, unless I had believed

That I would see the goodness of the Lord

In the land of the living.

Wait on the Lord;

Be of good courage,

And He shall strengthen your heart;

Wait, I say, on the Lord!"

God is our light and our strength. So, who shall we fear? If God is on our side, no enemy can overwhelm us, no disease can crush us, no fight can defeat us. God hides us away in the safety of His heart. In His heart, we are loved beyond imagining and carefully crafted for a purpose. We are strengthened and safe.

When an epidemic quickly escalated into a pandemic during 2020, you can easily imagine my fear of getting sick. The world was quarantined, and everyone was practicing social distancing.

There were so many stories about how the virus originated, how to avoid it, and what symptoms infected people might experience; it was hard to know what was true. Global chaos and confusion and fear abounded. So much fear.

I learned a lot during the coronavirus pandemic. One of the biggest lessons God taught me is this: patience is courage, and faith can overcome fear.

Quarantine was a time of waiting. Months of waiting to return to school and jobs and everyday life. Months of waiting to visit loved ones in person. Months of waiting to see if you would get sick and then waiting to heal if you did.

It takes a lot of courage to remain patient during such a fearful, chaotic season. It takes courage to care for sick family members and friends as you wait for them to heal. It takes courage to social distance and keep others safe when you feel so lonely. It takes courage to choose joy and choose Jesus no matter how long it takes for a trial to finish.

Quarantine was a season of fear, but it was also a season of faith. Psalm 27 tells us to wait on the Lord because He will strengthen our hearts. It takes courage to wait when you don't know what happens next. It takes faith to overcome the fear of the unknown.

When I felt scared and helpless during quarantine, God reminded me to seek His face. When we look for Him in difficult circumstances, He will reveal His presence, showing us that His everlasting light shines brightest when we choose to see Him.

The purpose of fear is for God to show us that there was never really anything to be afraid of in the first place. No matter how long we have to wait, how sick we get, or how helpless we feel, we can rest knowing there is nothing to fear because *God has already won.* He has defeated our enemies and brought us to peace. He has taught us to hope because of fear, not in spite of it. He has provided.

Purpose of Our Past

Just as God is the ultimate light to us, we are to reflect His light to others. Maybe you think you don't have any gifts or that God can't use you because of something you've done in your past. But believe me when I say this: God's light can only shine through us if we are broken first.

2 Corinthians 12:9 (ESV) says, "But he said to me, 'My grace is sufficient for you, for my power is made perfect in weakness.' Therefore, I will boast all the more gladly of my weaknesses, so that the power of Christ may rest upon me."

God's power is made perfect in our weakness. Everyone is broken. Everyone has a story to tell. *Brokenness is a gift.* It allows us to connect with the people around us, it allows heavenly light to shine through our brokenness, and it allows us to grow closer to God as His grace embraces us and His power fills us. What would the point of serving God be if we didn't need His forgiveness and love? God's power is made perfect in our weakness. Our weaknesses give us something to work toward, a goal to better ourselves, through mistakes and tears, yes, but also prayer and redemption. Our sins remind us of who the enemy is and inspire us to fight against our adversary the devil. Our past reminds us that we can overcome anything with God on our side.

The days we walk in sin are the days of mourning, and the only way to step into the joy of salvation is to praise God and live to serve Him. So when you question whether what you're doing is what the Lord wills for you, think about what really brings you joy. It's our Father, the everlasting light, and the days of idolizing anything else are over. As it's written in Isaiah, these moons no longer glow for us. These suns no longer beam for us. But God burns bright, our Everlasting Light, forever.

God breaks our hearts so that His light can shine through the cracks. The purpose of our past is to make us realize how far we've come: the beauty of our new lives compared to the darkness of our previous one. *The purpose of our past is to give us a story to share, a way to connect with others, an opportunity to bring people to Christ.* When we share our stories, God's light will shine through the cracks in our hearts and onto the lives of those around us, illuminating the glory of God that was there all along. Often, our hearts just have to break to see it.

Purpose of Hope

1 Peter 1:13 (NCV) says, "… All your hope should be for the gift of grace that will be yours when Jesus Christ is shown to you."

Sometimes our hearts have to break so we can see Jesus. Jesus knew great sorrow, but He also experienced immense joy and hope. Jesus's heart was broken many times, and it strengthened His faith. It gave Him a reason to hope for His Father in heaven. We can know if our hope is pure by our reaction to trials. If our hearts break and we remain hopeful, our hope is the true hope of God. But if our hearts break and our hope fails, we know it wasn't true hope.

Psalm 66:10 (ESV) puts it this way, "For you, O God, have tested us; you have tried us as silver is tried."

When our hearts break, not only does it help us determine if our hope is pure, but it helps us determine where we are in our relationship with God. If our hope is in Him unfailingly, we are in a good place. If our hope is wavering, we need to bring our doubts before Him so He can reassure us with gentle displays of His presence.

The purpose of hope is this: when our hearts break and we can't see what lies ahead, we know God will be with us. We must live expecting God to work in our lives and He will. If we have the hope of His presence in every moment of life, He will reveal Himself. We simply have to choose to hope, not in spite of our broken hearts, but because of them.

Once at my church, the older kids in the youth group joined the adults to learn about the early church and why we do the things we do. During one class, we discussed the Lord's Supper and what the Passover must have been like.

It must have felt strange to smear lamb's blood on their doors, to wonder if they did it right, if their firstborn child would perish before they woke up the next morning. There must have been so many mixed emotions. Fear, worry, uncertainty. Haste, sacrifice, nervousness. Excitement. Compassion for their children. Joy at God's presence and soon to be fulfilled promise. And the prominent emotion an unspoken presence in every home: a tentative hope that their God would finally deliver them from the hand of the Egyptians.

But unlike the Israelites, we shouldn't have a tentative hope. To live a life of everlasting light, we have to live a life of *certain* hope.

Even though the parent's hearts might have been breaking at the thought of losing their oldest child, those that took action to prevent death were hopeful. They believed that if they did what God told them to, He would protect and spare their child.

Even when our hearts are breaking, do we have hope that God will protect us, walk with us, and shine His light through our broken hearts the rest of the way to heaven?

Purpose of Struggling

More often than not, we have to struggle to grow. Struggling is not fun and never easy but who you'll be when you walk out of the storm is what's most important. We have to struggle to realize our full potential and become what God made us to be. Without struggling, there's no learning. Without struggling, there's no joy in success. Without struggling, there's nothing to work toward. Struggling means you're learning, and that God is shaping you into what He intended for your life. But when you struggle, don't turn against God—use it as an opportunity to grow closer to Him. Surrender to God. This battle of life is not for you to fight. Exodus 14:14 (NIV) reminds us, "The Lord will fight for you; you need only to be still."

The purpose of suffering is to show us God always has a plan, a good intention for our lives. It's to show us He had a plan all along; there was no need for worrying or anxiety or fear.

God will show you the way. He is near in our struggles, guiding us, teaching us, and loving us all the way through to the light of His joy and grace and purpose. Check out these verses and think about how struggling increases your strength and brings you closer to God:

- "Not only that, but we rejoice in our sufferings, knowing that suffering produces endurance, and endurance produces character, and character produces hope, and hope does not put us to shame, because God's love has been poured into our hearts through the Holy Spirit who has been given to us." (Romans 5:3-5 ESV)
- "And after you have suffered a little while, the God of all grace, who has called you to his eternal glory in Christ, will himself restore, confirm, strengthen, and establish you." (1 Peter 5:10 ESV)
- "For I know the plans I have for you, declares the Lord, plans for welfare and not for evil, to give you a future and a hope." (Jeremiah 29:11 ESV)
- "Some of the wise will stumble, so that they may be refined, purified and made spotless until the time of the end, for it will still come at the appointed time." (Daniel 11:35 NIV)
- **Bonus:** Check out the story of Jacob in Genesis 32:22-32. He wrestled with God and came out closer to Him than ever before. God uses our struggles to strengthen our faith and display His unlimited power and strength. Never forget that God doesn't waste our pain and that He uses our trials to teach us how to love Him more deeply. *This is one of the greatest gifts He could ever give us.*

Purpose of the Bible

The youth group piled into the church van, joking, laughing, and full of life, as we set off to the local soup kitchen. We signed the workers' forms, suited up in our aprons and gloves, and prepared lunch for the hungry and homeless people of our city. When everything was ready, the doors were opened, and people flooded in to hear a short devotional before the food was served.

The speaker was an elderly man and, if I remember correctly, he walked with a cane. He wore glasses, a hat with a dark green stripe around the middle, and a nice suit with a handkerchief that matched his tie. He rose humbly and slowly made his way to the front of the room. Speaking with great love and wonder about God's Word, he read many verses about what the Bible should mean to us (some of which I plan on sharing with you today) and repeated this simple but oh so powerful sentence over and over again: God's Word is precious.

He had the meek surety of an aging man who was used to being in front of audiences. Though his voice was not as strong as it once might have been, his love for God and for speaking and for the Bible had only seemed to grow over time. If I had to guess, I would say he used to be a preacher. Maybe he still is. But I never really got to know the man, and I don't know if I'll ever get to meet him again. If God arranges it, I will joyfully welcome the occasion as an opportunity to listen to his story and connect with a brother in Christ. If I could ask him one question, I would ask him what passage or verse in the Bible he has experienced in his life most wonderfully.

Although I may not know his answer to that question, I do know what the Bible means to him. To the old speaker, the Bible is precious, tender, lovely. It is a sign of God's love and goodness and wonder. It is a gift. It is to be used to draw nearer to our Creator, friend, and Father. It is to be used to learn how we can fulfill our purpose on Earth. Scripture sets an example for how we should live.

2 Timothy 3:16-17 (NIV) states, "All Scripture is God-breathed and is useful for teaching, rebuking, correcting and training in righteousness, so that the servant of God may be thoroughly equipped for every good work."

The Bible is inspired by God to inspire us. If we dive into its pages, meditating on its verses, God will show us how to teach ourselves and others, train to be righteous, serve on our knees, and most importantly, love sacrificially, endlessly, and unconditionally.

The Bible also proves God is real through true accounts of people who have experienced His love, mercy, wisdom, and power.

The Word shows that God keeps His promises and fulfills prophecies. The chance of all the prophecies and promises mentioned in the Bible being fulfilled is an insanely small amount. But everything single thing God said He would do, He did and is still doing now. There's no way any of it could have actually happened without God.

The Bible proves time and time again that God hears and answers prayers (Psalm 17:6), keeps His promises (Deuteronomy 28:9), and has a plan for us (Jeremiah 29:11). God provides the answers to our prayers through the Bible. His Word can reveal the answers to our next breakthrough. His Word can reveal how to push past our struggles, overcome our sins, and live a life fully dedicated to Him.

I asked some people what the Bible means to them, and this is how they answered:

- *The essence of who I am and why I am. (Nathan Lewis)*
- *A path God made so that people could be saved by His Word and Jesus's death. And we read it daily to know the guidelines of Christianity and what it means to love the Lord with all your soul. (Sarah Grace Young)*
- *The Bible is God's Word and His instructions for our lives. Every time I read it, I get reassurance, and I grow in my relationship with Him. I wish everybody had a copy to study and see all God has done for them. (Camryn Manly)*
- *The Bible heals you and it gives you hope and faith. The Bible is a book of answers, healing, and hope. It's a way you can talk to and connect with God. The Bible is a book of everyday guidance. It's uplifting and gives you peace and light and hope during dark times. (Sia Patel)*
- *The Bible is a living document of God's will. It is the foremost authority on how we, as Christians, should live, and it never becomes outdated. Its messages can always be applied in any age or time. (Seth Pratt)*
- *The Bible is not just a book you read for entertainment, it's a collection of history and truth. The Bible is filled with examples of how we need to follow God's Word and trust in Him through all of time. The Bible is a way of life. (Emma Gallagher)*

- *The Bible is a story of our people! God's people! The Bible reunites us together as one. It doesn't matter what religion or ethnicity you are. It shows the lessons God has taught others to teach us. The Bible is from God, and it shows its light in different ways every time I pick it up. (Hannah Lyons)*
- *The Bible. The Living Word of God. Sixty-six books wrapped in unfaltering prophetic love pointing to the cross. A love story. A compass for life that guides me in darkness, provides wisdom during my ignorance, and refocuses my thought process to that which pleases Christ. The Word is the bread I partake of in the early morning hour and the snack I chew upon between breaks on a busy day. His Word is the framework for your purpose in life. (Jah'Karious)*
- *The Bible helps guide me in how I conduct myself, handle life situations, and abide in Christ's love. It constantly reminds me of the life we are called to live and how God works in miraculous ways even when we may not see it. (Treava)*
- *The Bible is a book of instructions on how to live and love people. (Taylor Roberson)*
- *The Bible means everything to me! It's literally the Word of God that we have to guide us. A source of comfort in times when comfort is needed. (Matt Grinder)*

All these answers are so amazing, and I would like to share mine, too. To me, the Bible is open, relatable, and waiting. All we have to do is open its pages. The Bible is encouraging. It is a way of life. A way of living all in for God, a way of acting with divine purpose, a way of sharing the Good News to all we come in contact with. It's a way of praising God, developing a more intimate relationship with Him, and discerning what He is whispering to your heart.

If I had to pick one verse I have experienced in my life the most, it would be Psalm 30:5 (NKJV): "…Weeping may endure for a night, but joy comes in the morning."

The purpose of the Bible is for us to experience God in our lives and read His Word with a changed perspective. Every time we read it, we read it differently: we are constantly collecting new experiences. Reading a verse about joy before you've suffered heartbreak is not the same as reading a verse about joy after your heart has shattered multiple times.

It's amazing how we can look back and read Scripture through a new point of view, wondering at the power that rings from the perfection and truth of the words, falling in love with the God of stories all over again. Stories are so important to God—He gave us the Bible to connect with Him and with others through true accounts of His love. The Bible shows us that we are not alone and that we are understood and loved and have examples of faith to look back on and put into practice.

Stories are how we share the Good News, and the Bible tells the most important story of all: Jesus's story. That's what the whole Bible is about. It builds up to Jesus, tells of His life, and describes what happened after His death. It's all about Jesus. Everything in our lives should be about Jesus. Every decision, action, and word should all be for the glory of the one who sacrificed Himself for us.

We are fully known by God. That's why He gave us the Bible—*because He knows we need it.* The purpose of the Bible is to encourage us when we are weary, help us find our way when we are lost, and provide inspiration for fulfilling our purpose. But most of all, studying the Bible is about knowing God and learning to hear His voice. Then, you can share the story of not only Jesus but of how His sacrifice shines everlasting light into your life, overflowing your heart with love and gratitude and joy. *This* is what turns hearts to Christ.

Purpose of Life:
What Love Looks Like

I n my sophomore year, I wrote a play for theater class called *What Love Looks Like*. It's about two missionaries in Nicaragua. One feels as if he's had no impact during his time there, and the other reminds him that success isn't measured by how many meals you cook, how many houses you build, or how many people you provide for. It's not even about how many people were baptized. True success is measured by how many people we love. Love doesn't keep score of the good things you've done, and love doesn't do good things for others to see. Love is kind to bring glory to God and for no other reason. What does love look like to you? To me, love looks like answered prayers and friends who cry with you when you are sad. Love looks like Jesus dying on the cross to save us from our sins. Love looks like sacrifice and love looks like hope. Love is selfless and patient. Love is genuine. Love is everlasting. Think about how God has provided for you, open your heart and thank Him, and you will see what true love looks like as God works in your life like never before. I want you to know that I love you and will always be praying for you. Love never gives up. Don't forget how great God's love for you is. You are loved more than you can imagine. Keep going. You got this! The purpose of life is love. Many verses confirm this:

- *"Love is patient and kind; love does not envy or boast; it is not arrogant or rude. It does not insist on its own way; it is not irritable or resentful; it does not rejoice at wrongdoing but rejoices with the truth. Love bears all things, believes all things, hopes all things, endures all things. Love never ends..." (1 Corinthians 13:4-8 ESV)*
- *"For God so loved the world, that he gave his only Son, that whoever believes in him should not perish but have eternal life." (John 3:16 ESV)*
- *"Whoever confesses that Jesus is the Son of God, God abides in him, and he in God. So, we have come to know and to believe the love that God has for us. God is love, and whoever abides in love abides in God, and God abides in him." (1 John 4:15-16 ESV)*
- *"Let love be genuine. Abhor what is evil; hold fast to what is good." (Romans 12:9 ESV)*

Here is the play I wrote. I hope it will change your perspective on the purpose of life.

What Love Looks Like
By Lily K. Lewis

*(**P**aul walks onto the beach at sunrise, where he sees Adrian sitting on the black sand in deep concentration. Volcanoes can be seen in the background, along with the tiny houses the Nicaraguans live in and the church Adrian and Paul are staying at. Assuming he's praying, Adrian waits quietly for a few moments until he sees Paul look up.)*

PAUL: I love the black sand in Nicaragua. There's just something so wonderful about the ashes from a volcano being turned into something beautiful.

ADRIAN: You're right. I can't believe we have to leave in a few hours already. I feel like…
(Adrian sighs, gesturing for Paul to sit next to him.)

PAUL: I'm sad that we have to leave, too. I can feel the Lord's presence so strongly here. Everything is in clear focus. And the people… Helping them and seeing their joy in the Lord… Teaching the unbelievers who God is… *(Paul snaps his fingers when he says, "It's…" both times.)* Well, it's… it's… humbling.

ADRIAN (*Adrian gestures to the cardboard, tin homes, and trash lining the streets behind them.*): How can people who have so little and need so much have such great faith in the Lord?

(*Adrian runs his hands through his hair, obviously upset.*)

PAUL: I think this is more than just not wanting to leave. What's really bothering you?

ADRIAN: We didn't give those people any more reason to trust in the Lord. We were here for two months, and we were only able to build three tiny houses, provide a couple extra meals, and nobody was even baptized. Not one unbeliever was added to the church. Two months! And we accomplished nothing. I feel as if God isn't answering my prayers. I feel like He is distant. I know He's there. I *believe* it with all my heart. I just can't *feel* it in my heart.

(*Paul listens silently until Adrian is finished and then places a hand on his shoulder. Adrian has his head in his hands, eyes tearing up.*)

PAUL: Adrian, sit up. Look at me.

(*Adrian sits up but stares out at the ocean for a moment before meeting Paul's eyes.*)

PAUL: Success isn't measured by how many people we were able to help, how many wounds we were able to heal, or how many stomachs we were able to fill. It's not even measured by how many people were baptized. The true measure of success, not only for a mission trip but for *life*, is how many people you were able to show the love of Jesus.

(*Adrian blinks hard, as if in a daze. This thought had never occurred to him before.*)

PAUL: Who do you love, Adrian? The starving kids who play soccer in the streets? The children dreading the empty table awaiting them and their seven siblings in their one-room home?

(Adrian nods.)

PAUL: Who do you love, Adrian? The parents who want nothing more than to give their children a future but lack the means to provide it?

(Adrian has tears rolling down his cheeks now, but he manages another nod.)

PAUL: Who do you love, Adrian? The teenager who stole your wallet and the man who threatened you because you're a Christian?

ADRIAN: It wasn't easy, and it took many years to learn how to forgive but... yes. Through the many trials I have faced, God has shown me that I need to see others the way He does, looking at what they can be and not at what they are or were. We all make mistakes, but often God takes our mistakes and turns them into something more beautiful than we ever could have imagined. I mean, who knew that by getting my wallet stolen, I'd learn a lesson about compassion?

(Paul nods in agreement, a small smile on his face as he remembers when Adrian's wallet was stolen.)

PAUL: Who do you love, Adrian? The unbelievers, the persecutors, and the lost?

ADRIAN: Yes, absolutely, all of them.

PAUL: Who do you love, Adrian? Do you love the Lord?

ADRIAN: I love the Lord with everything I am and all that I hope to be.

PAUL *(Paul abruptly changes the subject.)*: While we've been in Nicaragua, how many people have you hugged?

(This startles a laugh out of Adrian. He looks surprised to be laughing himself. This makes Paul smile.)

ADRIAN: With their custom of hugging every person they meet... at least a hundred.

PAUL: How many people have you listened to when they were hurting?

ADRIAN: Quite a few.
(Adrian laughs to himself, shaking his head.)

PAUL: How many hands have you held as someone passed away, praying over them and for their families? How many mourners have you comforted with promises from God's Word?

ADRIAN: About three.

PAUL: Have you loved others like God loves you and them and all creation?

ADRIAN: I have tried my best every day to love like Jesus. I have failed many times, but I have always tried.
(Paul nods in agreement before speaking.)

PAUL: That's all God is asking you to do—to show them what His love looks like. *(Paul looks at the ground and then at the sunrise in front of them as he speaks, not making eye contact. He seems to have difficulty speaking because he is emotional. He clears his throat before continuing.)* May I share something with you?

ADRIAN *(Adrian places a hand on Paul's shoulder.)*: Of course.

PAUL: You know what my home life was like before I came to college with you. My parents were abusive, and there were many nights I wanted to run away or give up. I didn't grow up in the church; I didn't know how to show others kindness because I had never been shown kindness myself. I was addicted to drugs and spent my nights drunk and smoking at parties, all the while feeling dead inside. But when I met you, you shared the Good News with me, the Good News about Jesus and how He died on the cross so that we could be free from sin. You showed me how to be kind. You showed me what the love of Jesus looks like. When I was ready, I wanted you to baptize me because God used you to bring me to Him. From that day on, we have been best friends, serving the Lord together wherever we go. Perhaps God sent you to bring me to Him first. But maybe God brought us together so I could help you, too. Earlier, you asked how people who have so little and need so much could have such great faith. The answer is hope. The answer is love. Because they hope in the Lord, He strengthens and guides them. Because they love God, He guards their hearts from fear and envelops them with peace. Don't lose hope, Adrian. I know God will work through this pain. I know that He *is* working. *Right now.* Even though it seems impossible, God is working, and He is near, and He is good.

(Both Adrian and Paul are crying now.)

ADRIAN: I never knew I had that great of an impact on you—all because I chose to love like Jesus.

PAUL: It's true.
(Paul glances at his watch.)

PAUL: Well, I guess we better go get packed and start heading toward the airport. It's about an hour from León to Managua, and the plane starts boarding in six hours.

ADRIAN: You're right. We should go.

(They stand up and exchange a brief hug. As they turn to start walking back toward their house, wiping their eyes, they notice someone running toward them from the direction of the church. Paul and Adrian squint and shield their eyes with their hands, attempting to discern the figure.)

ADRIAN: Hey, is that Sandra?

PAUL: I think so. And it sounds like she's calling our names.
(Sandra, a member of the church, enters the stage. She is out of breath as she speaks.)

ADRIAN: Is everything okay, Sandra? What happened?
(Sandra smiles.)

SANDRA: I'm so glad I caught you guys before you left. I have some fantastic news. My son wants to get baptized! Juan wants to live for the Lord!
(Adrian and Paul exchange glances.)

PAUL: God sure does work in amazing ways sometimes.

ADRIAN: Ain't that the truth.
(Sandra gives them a questioning look.)

SANDRA: Did I miss something?
(Adrian and Paul make eye contact again and laugh.)

PAUL: Not much.
(Sandra shrugs with a knowing smile. Juan enters the stage. Everyone embraces Juan one at a time. Adrian ruffles his hair, Paul gives him a high-five, and Sandra kisses him on both cheeks.)

SANDRA (*Sandra holds Juan's shoulders at an arm's length away*): Would you like Paul or Adrian to baptize you, Juan?
(*Juan smiles from ear to ear.*)

JUAN: I would like Paul to baptize me.
(Paul looks surprised. This will be the first person he has ever baptized, though he knows the words by heart.)

PAUL: Nothing would bring me greater joy.
(*Adrian smiles at Juan and Paul as they wade into the ocean. Sandra speaks to Adrian.*)

SANDRA: I'm so proud of both of them.

ADRIAN: Me too, Sandra. Me, too.
(*Paul and Juan are now about waist-deep in the water.*)

PAUL: Do you, Juan, believe that Jesus Christ is the Son of God?

JUAN: I do.

PAUL: I will now baptize you in the name of the Father, and the Son, and the Holy Spirit.
(*Juan holds his nose, and Paul places his hand over Juan's, submerging him completely under the water before pulling him back up. They embrace and then walk back toward the shore. Adrian, Sandra, Juan, and Paul hold hands and bow their heads as Paul leads a prayer.*)

PAUL: Dear Lord, You have provided. When we needed You most, when we were discouraged, You showed us what Your love looks like. Your love is compassionate and kind and forgiving. Your love is comforting and understanding. Your love is true. Your love is abundant. Your love is everlasting, as is our purpose to love others. Please help Juan, and all believers, to feel and show this love every day of their lives. Amen.

(Adrian, Juan, and Sandra repeat "Amen" in unison. When they break the huddle, they see a few friends have gathered behind them.)

ADRIAN: Hey! What are you guys here for?

SANDRA *(Sandra smiles softly.)*: They're here to say goodbye.

FRIENDS: We love you! You guys are awesome. We will continue praying for you daily, dear friends. Thank you. You have been a great help to us. We will never forget you.

(Adrian and Paul smile and embrace their friends, eyes brimming with tears, overcome with joy and thankfulness. Everyone freezes. A spotlight shines on Adrian; he looks toward the audience but above their heads and closes his eyes.)

ADRIAN: Thank You, Lord. *(Adrian opens his eyes and looks at his friend who helped him through so much. Love and thankfulness shine in the eyes of the group, and Adrian smiles, joyful, humbled, and thankful.)* Now this is what love looks like. *(Adrian looks up and smiles. Lights go black. Curtain closes.)*

Part Five:

Can He Still Feel the Nails?

Can He Still Feel the Nails

by Ray Boltz

Can He still feel the nails every time I fail?
Can He hear the crowds cry crucify again?
Am I causing Him pain
When I know I've got to change?
Cause' I just can't bear the thought of hurting Him
Holy, Holy, Holy is the Lamb.
Holy, Holy, Holy is the Lamb.

The Way We Live

"First I preached to the people in Damascus, and then I went to Jerusalem and all over Judea. Finally, I went to the Gentiles and said, 'Stop sinning and turn to God! Then prove what you have done by the way you live.'" (Acts 26:20 CEV)

When we repent, are baptized, and then forgiven, our lives should be transformed. Are we living like God is our everlasting light?

Okay, you guys. Let's be honest: we all get a little grumpy sometimes. Every once in a while, all the things in our lives just become so overwhelming, and we don't know how to handle it, so we take it out on others. We've all said things we regret. We all sometimes wish we had been nicer, braver, or wiser at some point in our lives. Often, the way we live is not the way we should be living. We walk around with our eyes and hearts closed to God and wonder why we never see or hear from Him anymore. This happens to all of us at different times in our lives.

It happened fairly recently for me, but one song changed everything: "A Common Love." This song means more to me than I can explain; it always uplifts me and reminds me of some of my most joyful memories. I poured out my heart, and God filled my soul with joy and hope and love. Together we sang,

"A common love for each other
A common gift to the Savior
A common bond holding us to the Lord.
A common strength when we're weary
A common hope for tomorrow,
A common joy in the truth of God's word."

At the end of the song, I opened my eyes, and everything was clearer than before.

I saw, for the first time in a while, the beauty and wonder of the people God created around me and the unbreakable connection of the common love we shared. I could see the love in the room. I felt it in my heart, offering it to all those around me so they might see the bond uniting us too. Love is meant to be shared. Don't keep it to yourself.

If the way you live stops you from sharing love with all those you encounter, you're never going to see the world clearly. If you live without love at all, it's like your eyes are closed; you'll never see the wonderful things God has in store for you until you open them.

In the moments after the song, when I had opened my eyes, I remembered the sunset prayer walks I had recently taken. It was the end of winter; spring peeked out from around the corner. At first, as I searched for signs of spring, I was pleased to find a green patch of grass on my walks. One day, suddenly, I realized there were flowers and trees and green, green grass all around me. I was overwhelmed with God's love and the warmth of the creation that surrounded me. Are you searching for patches of grass, or are you searching for a road lined with flowers? When we live in a way that actively seeks out God, God will reveal Himself; He will provide. We simply have to look. Are you living in a way that doesn't even get close to reaching your full potential? Is the way you live beautiful and satisfying and God-filled? If it's not, remember to start by searching for the greenest patch of grass and work up from there until the glory of spring surrounds you.

Immutable Determination

I have visited Nicaragua two times on separate mission trips. It is the most beautiful place I have ever been. It's not the volcanos or the black sand beaches that make it so wonderful. It's the way the sunset seems more vibrant when I'm in the presence of the Lord like never before, surrounded by people determined to love as Jesus did like no one I've ever met. Even in the face of starvation and sickness and so, so much need, they are determined to give generously. Like so many godly characters in the Bible, the Christians of Nicaragua are willing to give up their lives for God. If that means caring for the sick or feeding the hungry at their own expense, it doesn't matter, because all that's important to them is showing love to others.

In Nicaragua there are no cold greetings or unacknowledged blessings. There is no fear or doubt. There is only love and God and light.

This is a poem I wrote in admiration of the resilience of the Nicaraguan people called "Until They Lay Down":

Until They Lay Down

Dawn breaks, spreading warmth over the restless ocean,
Waves cresting and crashing pearl,
Stark against the black sand beach.
One-room homes with tin roofs, dirt floors line the street,
Housing families of seven.
Men and children weave through the tangle of traffic,
Baskets balanced atop their heads,
Selling anything to feed their families.
Along the rough road, if you look to your right,
You'll notice a volcano looming high and proud,
Piercing the merciless sun.
Smoke curls from the top,
The yowl of a bone-thin dog.
Feral, unfeeling. A threat, taunting,
"Perhaps today I will take everything away,
Though there's not much to burn."
The Nica people refuse to fear.
Enduring, resilient. Strength evident
As they scrub clothes clean against rocks in a polluted river,
They look up and smile.
Without bitterness, with gratitude,
They give thanks to God for all He has blessed them with.
Even as they starve, scraping for a handful of rice,
They always have room for a guest at their table.
From the oldest woman, not yet sixty,
To the youngest babe,
A kiss on the cheek and the warmest embrace
Replace cold greetings.
When the faintest red tints the edges of the sky,
Slowly, slowly,

Fire consumes the evening.

Quick as a strike of lighting, smooth as precious rain,

Darkness smothers the fire, every flame turned to ash,

Stars pricking the silky black fabric

Like a million gleaming needles.

People flood the square, dancing, singing, drunk and rejoicing.

Rebelling, until they lay down.

They rise in the morning, light shining along

the planes of their work-worn faces.

Preparing for the day, same as all that came before,

They make a promise to themselves and to each other.

To fight for better

Until they lay down.

Are you fighting for better? Are you determined to show others God's love no matter the cost? In order to live a life of everlasting light, we have to live a life of determination. Do you give up when loving others becomes too hard? I have learned so much from the Nicaraguans. They inspire me to be more thankful, more giving, and more determined. They inspire me to love. But most of all, they inspire me to be resilient in hope.

When a dearly beloved friend and preacher, Armando, passed away from COVID, my heart was broken. I fell to my knees; I prayed, asking God, "Why? Every day someone I love is dying or hurt or sick. I can't catch a break. Sorrow is chasing me around while I'm chasing joy. How can I keep going if things only get harder and harder and harder? When will I finally snap for good—broken beyond repair?"

As I sobbed on the floor beside my bed, a gift from Armando clutched against my chest, I remembered the resilience of the Nicaraguan people and changed my prayer. "God, I may not understand what's happening, but what I do know is that You are good and that You have a plan. It's not about me—it's about bringing glory to You. Help me to be strong. Help me to be as determined as the Nicaraguans. Comfort me, Lord, and his family. I beg you, God. Teach us to hope again, more deeply. Help us."

I chose to hope and to trust in God, even as my heart broke yet again, because I know He has a plan. I know I can find the light in this situation if I search for it relentlessly. And I believe that my God, my tender and merciful Prince of Peace, is always, always good, no matter what happens.

When I am struggling, I will remember that I can trust in God no matter the circumstance, just like the Nicaraguans. Whatever they are facing, they do not turn away from Him. No matter how dark it is, no matter how long until morning comes, they hope in God's everlasting light. He is the light that shines in the darkness, the joy that carries us forward. God is our strength and our peace and our comfort. He is our Father and friend. He is our hope.

I pray that you will be filled with the determination to keep hoping no matter what you encounter. If you fill your life with God's light, you will never be in darkness. If you are suffering and sick and weary and tired, there is hope. If you are hurting, lost and confused and alone, God is with you. If you have sinned and long to come home, God loves you and frees you from your sorrow. If you have found your purpose, to love others and bring God glory, there is light. There is an everlasting light that will never die out. All you have to do is hope in God alone, and there will be no darkness. All you have to do is believe, and God will always pull you through, stronger than ever before. All you have to do is love, and you will find joy. *Follow God-inspired, determined, and relentless, and you will have a life of everlasting light.* And never forget to watch for a beautiful, humbling sunset—God might just speak to your heart through it.

"Weeping may endure for a night, but joy comes in
the morning." (Psalm 30:5 NKJV) Amen.

Persistent Obedience

Young Life club, a program through which leaders reach out to high school kids to teach them about God's Word, is held at a different location every week. We draw tickets for raffle prizes and dress up for a theme. We sing fun karaoke songs, and later we pour out praise to God. At the end, we have a short devotional thought that never ceases to help me walk with confidence in the Lord.

The leader for my age group, Treava, holds a Bible study for our group of girls called Campaigners. We meet once a week to encourage each other and dive deeper into God's Word. The past few weeks, we've been reading *What Happens When Women Say Yes to God* by Lysa TerKeurst. In the opening chapter, the author shares the story of how God encouraged her to give her Bible to a stranger on a plane. Despite her reluctance, she obeyed, and God worked wonders from there. The man she gave the Bible to, who knew nothing about God, *took a week off work to read the Bible.* He decided to visit a church, and accidentally ended up at the author's church.

God does amazing things when we simply set aside our selfish excuses and say, "Yes, God. I am willing."

As soon as Treava finished reading, I knew what I had to do. I had been meaning to buy a Bible for a friend who needed one, and I still had just not gotten around to it. I made excuses like not having the time or energy or money. I told myself I would go and get the Bible when I could drive in a couple short weeks. My parents were tired of driving me around, and I didn't want to ask. When I finally got my driver's license, I still didn't go. More excuses; not enough time. It was selfish. But hearing the story of how the author had been willing to say yes to God, I decided to say yes and see what would happen.

As soon as we finished, I grabbed my keys, drove to the bookstore, and bought the Bible. I no longer cared about the price or the time or the energy it took. I just cared about saying yes to God. I brought the Bible to my friend the next day, and she was extremely touched; we started studying the Bible together. The story of how she went from not having a relationship with God to having a beautiful faith reminds me of how important saying yes to God is. If we want to live a life of everlasting light, we have to live a life of everlasting obedience.

Notice I didn't say we have to live a life of everlasting obedience as long as it's comfortable, popular, and easy. Living obediently will often cause you to crawl out of your comfort zone. Whether it be standing up to friends who are doing the wrong things, sitting with the "uncool" kid at lunch, or buying a Bible for a friend, living obediently takes courage.

If we already plan on saying no to God before He even asks us to do something, how can we ever grow closer to Him? Although it may be awkward or nerve-racking or scary, we have to say yes. *Just like how the author's story inspired me, your story of everlasting obedience may inspire someone else.*

If we wait too long to say yes to God, we may miss opportunities. Others will follow your example. *Your story can inspire others.* Say yes to God, so He can fill your life with the everlasting light of joy beyond imagining.

Continual Mercy: A Meditation of Psalm 136

This chapter is a guided meditation of Psalm 136 (NKJV). I want you to remember these words as you read the following verses: God is good, His mercy is great, and we have every reason to thank Him every waking moment of our lives, not in spite of what we are going through, but because what we are facing makes us stronger. Can I get an amen from the back?

"Oh, give thanks to the Lord, for He is good!
For His mercy endures forever.
Oh, give thanks to the God of gods!
For His mercy endures forever.

Oh, give thanks to the Lord of lords!
For His mercy endures forever:
To Him who alone does great wonders,
For His mercy endures forever;
To Him who by wisdom made the heavens,
For His mercy endures forever;
To Him who laid out the earth above the waters,
For His mercy endures forever;
To Him who made the great lights,
For His mercy endures forever—
The sun to rule by day,
For His mercy endures forever;
The moon and stars to rule by night,
For His mercy endures forever.
To Him who struck Egypt in their firstborn,
For His mercy endures forever;
And brought out Israel from among them,
For His mercy endures forever;
With a strong hand and with an outstretched arm,
For His mercy endures forever;
To Him who divided the Red Sea in two,
For His mercy endures forever;
And made Israel pass through the midst of it,
For His mercy endures forever;
But overthrew Pharoah and his army in the Red Sea,
For His mercy endures forever;
To Him who led His people through the wilderness,
For His mercy endures forever;
To Him who struck down great kings,
For His mercy endures forever;
And slew famous kings,

For His mercy endures forever;

Sihon king of the Amorites,

For His mercy endures forever;

And Og king of Bashan,

For His mercy endures forever—

And gave their land as a heritage,

For His mercy endures forever;

A heritage to Israel His servant,

For His mercy endures forever;

Who remembered us in our lowly state,

For His mercy endures forever;

And rescued us from our enemies,

For His mercy endures forever;

Who gives food to all flesh,

For His mercy endures forever;

Oh, give thanks to the God of heaven!

For His mercy endures forever."

Every day we will make mistakes, and every day we will fail. We will stumble and fall and pull ourselves up with the strength of the Lord. We will cry and hurt and hurt others, sometimes intentionally, sometimes unintentionally. We will lie and cheat and covet. We will lust after things we shouldn't, and we will get distracted.

We are human and God understands. He knows we will mess up. He knows we are going to fall—that's why He's there to pick us right back up. God knows we are going to sin. He doesn't expect us to be perfect, but He does expect us to make an effort.

There is an extreme difference between trying to follow God and sinning and not trying to follow God and sinning. God's mercy endures forever but remember to work hard to live in the way God has called you to. Only then will you experience everlasting light for eternity.

Paper Bag Speech

In the second semester of my sophomore year, I finally got to have Mrs. Billingsley, whose Speech class I had been eagerly looking forward to. She helped me with a lot of creative writing competitions in my freshman year by giving me some really helpful tips and just encouraging me throughout the whole process. She is so fun to be around; she always brightens a room with her wide smile and kind words. She's the type of teacher that reminds me why I love to learn.

On the first day of class after Christmas break, we were assigned to write a "paper bag speech" and then read it to the class the next day. This assignment involved choosing three items that can fit inside a paper bag that provide a glimpse into who you are and explaining why you chose those three things.

As I thought about what items to include in my paper bag speech, I realized I couldn't figure out anything to put in my bag that didn't involve God in some way. If the speech were to effectively show a part of who I am, the objects would all have to have something to do with God. God has become an inextricable part of who I am. Without Him, I have no idea who I would be. My life would be empty. I would be without passion, without vibrance. *If you want to live a life of everlasting light, God must become a fundamental part of what makes you* you.

My youth minister once challenged us with this question: If you stopped being a Christian today, would anyone notice?

When you hear this, what is your first response? What is your honest answer? If the answer is no, then maybe you should rethink the way you've been living. If the answer is yes, don't ever give up. True life is the best life, and I desire with all my heart for each and every one of you, dear readers, to discover and experience God fully as you open your heart to Him more and more.

I decided to structure my speech in a way that slowly leads the listeners deeper into who I am. As with most initial interactions, I started with surface-level adjectives of myself and listed the things I love. I stated things most people would know about me—things that were obvious. But as I dove deeper, down into the next paragraph, I began to open my heart little by little. I explained *why* I love the things I love, what I longed for, and one of the times I feel closest to God.

For my final paragraph, I laid my heart bare and tried to share the most profound piece of myself: the place where God lives in my heart, filling me with light and wonder. As I prepared to share this speech with the class, I was a little nervous. I wasn't scared of standing in front of people, but of being completely honest about who I am. I'm not ashamed of who I am, but something about being vulnerable with people hasn't always come naturally to me. However, I knew God was calling me out of my comfort zone; where He beckons I will follow, even if I don't understand why, even if I don't want to, even if I'm scared. I know His plan is better than mine. And so, with trust in my heart after praying for God to fill me with confidence and hope that my speech might touch the lives of those around me, I took my spot at the front, pulling the three objects from my paper bag, and began to read:

Paper Bag Speech

The first item I chose to put in my paper bag is a pair of socks with books on them. This embodies my love of reading, writing, and tacky socks, which perfectly corresponds with my personality. They also represent my love of soccer because I wear them to practice. They remind me of camp, which has helped make me who I am, and I wear them for tacky day or if I'm feeling spicy, with sandals. It's not so much the socks that matter, but the memories I've made while wearing them.

The second item I placed in my paper bag is a painting I bought from a souvenir shop in Nicaragua while on a mission trip. This represents my love of travel and my dream to become a missionary and a writer. The painting contains rich, deep colors in the volcanos and ocean and flora that invoke the imagination and make me long to be on an adventure just like the people rowing the boats. Also depicted in the painting is a warm sunset with quieter, softer hues. This represents my love of sunsets, born of the desire to find God in His marvelous creation. It's my favorite time to walk or run every day, because it serves as inspiration for some of my best writing.

The third item in my paper bag is a flower. This represents how I can find wonder in even the smallest of God's creations. The complexity and beauty of the flower is wonderful, and it's astonishing to think about the countless number of daisies, sunflowers, and lilies on this earth, each crafted and formed by God so carefully, so lovingly. It reminds me of the many times people have offered me flowers: when I was sick to cheer me up, when I was going to a dance to match my dress, when I was the flower girl in a wedding to toss petals and prepare the way for the bride.

Flowers seem to make sorrowful situations brighter and joyful situations even more thrilling.

As I silently prayed to God at my desk before it was my turn to speak, the girl who went before me, a sweet, gentle soul named Eliza, used her Bible as one of the objects in her speech. She talked about how important it was to her because she's a Christian. Eliza said she and her mother were challenging each other to read the Bible in a year. Immediately, I felt the Holy Spirit tapping on my heart. I was inspired by her courage. I prayed for confidence, and God provided in the form of Eliza, a dear friend who was unafraid to share her faith.

After class, as we walked to our next block, I told her I was also reading the Bible in a year, and I was only eleven days from finishing. We talked about the different difficulties it presents and how to overcome them. She asked if I would help keep her accountable, and I was so happy I could help in some small way. I told her how proud I was of her, and my heart overflowed with joy. I felt the Holy Spirit tapping on my heart again, and I knew what I had to do.

Through this, God answered more than one prayer. Not only did He answer my plea for confidence and courage, but He gave me the opportunity to be a light at school. Even more than that, He confirmed that something I wanted to do was something that *He* wanted me to do.

The first chapter of *What Happens When Women Say Yes to God* by Lysa TerKeurst, talks about how God called her to give her Bible to a stranger on a plane. She did, and wonderful results ensued.

After seeing this, I knew that after I finished reading my Bible, I wanted to pass it on and challenge someone else to read it in a year and then pass it on and so forth. I prayed God would provide the right person, someone who would really accept the challenge. When Eliza told me that she often struggled to keep track of what days to read what, I knew she was the one God wanted me to give my Bible to. It was organized into different readings by date, and I just knew she would love it. I determined to give it to her as soon as I finished. God answered my prayers and He provided abundantly. Everlasting light often looks like overflowing prayers and experiencing God in all our interactions.

God continued to amaze me with answered prayers later that afternoon in the car. I found out Mrs. Billingsley had emailed my mom to tell her what a good job I had done with my paper bag speech. I shared my speech with my mom because she's always really helpful, and I need someone to do some hard editing, but I knew there was one thing she wouldn't like: the last sentence.

Typically, a closing sentence is intended to summarize a speech or essay or whatever you are presenting, but for this particular project, I decided to do a little something different. I ended with a sentence that added detail to the last paragraph without explicitly closing the speech with a conclusion or summary.

It took me a while to finally understand why I wrote it the way I did. I'm thankful she really challenged me to think about it. I chose an unusual ending because I didn't really want to end the speech. The speech is about who I am and the things that represent me, but I'm not done growing into who I am becoming yet. By leaving the speech in some ways incomplete, I tried to convey the parts of my life that are not yet filled, the experiences and wisdom I must gain and the prayers I must pray before I become who God made me to be, living up to all His plans and my full potential through saying yes to Christ. It also represents the part of me that wouldn't be complete without God—it represents who I could've been and who I strive not to be.

True life is about viewing all of our experiences as opportunities to grow closer to God and recognizing Him in all the moments and encounters in our lives, big or small. I mean, think about it. It's awesome how a gift of silly socks from a friend can end up in a chapter of a book because it helped to teach me something about God. He really works in astounding ways sometimes. He answers our pleas in forms we never expect. Through this speech, God answered many prayers. He helped me to be open and courageous. He gave me an opportunity to help a friend. He provided the right person to offer my Bible to. And through the conversation with my mom, He answered my prayer of understanding who I am and why I write the way I do, what influences me, what drives me. He helped me become a better writer by challenging me to think about what I'm writing.

I prayed to discover who I am, and God's answer came in the form of a realization: *I don't know who I would be without God. Do you?*

I'm thankful God took a situation where I might normally lose my patience and turned it into an opportunity to grow closer to Him. Praise the Lord!

Part Six:

Rise, Let Us Go from Here

We Will Stand

by Russ Taff

Oh, you're my brother, you're my sister
So take me by the hand.
Together we will work until He comes again.
There's no foe that can defeat us
When we're walking side by side.
We will overcome the darkness,
Shine His light across this land.
As long as there is love, we will stand.

The Father's House

While I was studying and writing up a storm during my Freshman year English class, little did I know that a girl named Sia was beginning to wonder who God was. Before reading an excerpt from *Night* by Elie Wiesel, she had never really heard about God. Her parents were from India and her whole family was Hindu. But as we read from *Night*, she became more and more curious.

My friend Camryn was Sia's partner in class, and Sia, knowing Camryn was a Christian, began asking Camryn about God—who He is, what He does, where He can be found. Meanwhile, I sat across the room, oblivious to the miracle happening right in front of me.

Camryn brought Sia a Bible, and they began to study it together, listening to worship music and talking about Jesus and how He can help them through the toughest situations, how He is an everlasting light to those who struggle with anxiety and fear.

I remained clueless until a few months later during the coronavirus pandemic. Camryn texted me and asked if I would start doing Bible studies with her and Sia because she needed help answering some of the tough questions Sia was asking. I immediately agreed, confident that although I may not have all the answers, God would provide the words.

They told me about how Sia had come to learn about Christ, and I was astounded. Astounded that I hadn't noticed. Astounded by Camryn's witness to Sia. Astounded by the love that poured from both of them and astounded that God had given me the opportunity to be a part of such a beautiful story.

We began meeting at a coffee shop to study God's Word. When we weren't able to meet in person—none of us had a car at the time—we would Facetime, learning and asking questions together.

A wonderful friendship formed between the three of us. I was honored to call Camryn, lovely, kind, God-fearing Camryn, my friend. I admired her boldness and her willingness to say yes to God. I was thrilled to find a new friend in Sia, who has a beautiful smile and a really big heart. I was so excited to see their love for Christ grow by the day.

After a couple months and many Bible studies, Sia decided she was ready to be baptized. I cried when I heard the news. I was overjoyed by this gift God had gifted me and Camryn, the gift of seeing a wonderful friend find Jesus and choose to live for Him. And the gift God had given Sia: the gift of new life. Again, I was astounded that God continued to provide abundantly. He never ceases to amaze or surprise me.

The night before her baptism, she was so nervous, but she was even more excited. We talked with her and prayed with her, and her heart was comforted.

The next morning, we all met at Sia's church, and our Young Life leader, Treava, joined us. As I watched Sia get baptized, I was moved to tears again. I poured out every bit of my joy and praise into a song for our merciful Savior.

The song we sang, "Father's House" by Cory Asbury, goes a little something like this,

"Sometimes on this journey, I get lost in my mistakes
What looks to me like weakness is a canvas for Your strength
And my story isn't over, my story's just begun
Failure won't define me cause' that's what my Father does
Ooh, lay your burdens down
Check your shame at the door (ooh)
'Cause it ain't welcome anymore (ooh)
Ooh, you're in the Father's house."

As we sang, I felt the words. We can't get lost in our mistakes or our past. When we are made new, our sins are forgiven, and we have a new life, a life spent living for Jesus, and what happened before doesn't matter anymore. Our story starts when we choose to die to ourselves and our old ways and be baptized into true life with Christ. That's the day we start living, the day we become alive.

Failure doesn't define you or me. The past is behind us. All that lay before us is God if we choose to pay attention and seek His everlasting light.

As the song led into the chorus, I was reminded that when you are baptized you leave whatever shame you were carrying in your life before behind you. You're in the Father's house, and in the Father's house there are no burdens; there is no more shame. There is only hope and love, joy and light.

I looked over to see Sia standing next to Camryn with tears streaming down her cheeks. I could see she had been made light by the power of Jesus's forgiveness. I could feel her joy, could hear it in her song, could see it in her tears and hands raised to heaven.

I thought about Sia's journey to where she stood right now, made new through Jesus's blood, and a new wave of praise to God crashed over my heart, caressed my soul. The journey is what made this moment so wonderful. The journey is what changes us into who God intended us to be, no matter the ending.

God doesn't want perfect. He just wants our love. If we love Him, everything will work out for good in the end. Romans 8:28 (NKJV) promises, "And we know that all things work together for good to those who love God, to those who are called according to His purpose."

Failures, with God on our side, are just another journey in which to find Him, just another way for us to grow closer to Him. God transforms our failures into success when we choose to view our circumstances with a heavenly perspective. There is no more failure in the Father's house. Only triumph through Christ Jesus.

My lips curved into a smile as the second verse bled into the chorus.

Let go of your shame. Let go and enter the Father's house. Let go and choose eternal life through baptism. Lay your burdens down. Lay them down and enter the Father's house. Lay them down and don't look back.

I could feel God's presence in the room. God is good. God is love. Choose to let Him bring you home. All you have to do to enter the Father's house is say yes to God. Say yes. Please, *say yes.*

God's love overwhelmed me in this exquisite moment, this beautiful song. The Father was in the room in our English class, and He is in the room wherever you are right now. Close your eyes, open your heart. Listen. *You will hear Him when You believe.*

I believed.

There is nothing God cannot do, nothing He will not do when You ask something of Him according to His will with pure intentions in faith. I prayed for God to amaze me, and He provided abundantly.

My hands were palm up to God as we sang, and I *felt* the words. There's no reason for anxiety or fear. We're in the Father's House. There's so much love all around. We're in the Father's House. We lay our burdens down and we are made light. We're in the Father's House. We are baptized; we are made new. We're in the Father's House. We're in the Father's House.

Isaiah 57:14-15 (NCV) says, "Someone will say, 'Build a road! Build a road! Prepare the way! Make the way clear for my people.' And this is the reason: God lives forever and is holy. He is high and lifted up. He says, 'I live in a high and holy place, but I also live with people who are sad and humble. I give new life to those who are humble and to those whose hearts are broken.'"

Wherever we are in body, the Father is in the room. Wherever we are in spirit, whether we are lost, broken, or ashamed, God is at the door to take all that away. He is in the room to bring you new life, to work miracles, to give you hope, and to show you what His immortal love can do.

God is shining His everlasting light right in front of us, miracles are happening before our eyes, yet we are oblivious. We have to choose to pay attention. We have to choose to see what's happening around us, good or bad, and praise God.

Wherever we are, we are in the Father's house. Live every moment full of love, without shame. We're in the Father's house. Rise, let us go from this place of sin and into a life spent with Jesus. Rise, let us go from our state of shame. Rise, let us enter the Father's House. He is waiting with open arms. *He is waiting for you to come home.*

Overseer of Our Souls

J esus is the Overseer of our souls, and we are the sheep who need His constant guidance and comfort, watching us throughout the night and protecting us from evil things lurking in the shadows. In the same way, Jesus watches over us; He sends people out into the world to guide others as leaders and friends and confidantes. He sends these people as a gift, as a mouthpiece for His will.

I am lucky to have had many people sent from God in my life. So many friends and speakers and strangers. I am also fortunate to have been that person for some people. God answered my prayer of being a light by sending me to encourage and help these people with the wisdom He alone could provide through the various sufferings and challenges I've endured. I've learned to be thankful for suffering and welcome challenges for that very reason: to give me more ways to connect with others. *The more that I've gone through, the more I can help others get through by the grace of Jesus Christ.* The more that I've been challenged, the more I can show others how to come out stronger. The more I grow closer to God, the better I can live as an example.

Sometimes when we are distracted or hurting, the best thing we can do is focus on others. Don't get me wrong. It's essential to take care of your spiritual life first, praying and asking God for help, but sometimes healing takes shared experiences and suffering. When we let go of our distractions and choose to seek peace through helping others, we will discover a new type of healing: connection.

The connections we can form through shared wounds will have an everlasting impact on your heart. By going through the process of healing hand in hand, you form a bond through Jesus Christ that cannot be broken. The friends who stick with us through the messy days and weeks and years are the friends we should trust the most, the friends we would do anything for. By confiding in one another and focusing on each other during common trials, our own anxiety will fall away, and we can better bring glory to God.

We have to rise from our place of pain and go help others in order to heal. It's this connection that sparks unending, everlasting light in our lives.

The Sun Goes Down

When anger is described, it is often expressed as a burning sensation. I've found this to be so true. I've been so angry that I couldn't breathe. I've been so furious that my chest felt seared by its fire. I've been so mad that all I could do was cry. Yes, I once struggled with so, so much anger. But, it was only through a lot of praying, reading my Bible, and discovering who I am and who I want to be, that enabled me to overcome the burning in my soul.

In this chapter, I want to provide a list of steps and some tips that can help you overcome your anger:

1. The first part of overcoming anger is *deciding* to overcome your anger.

What I've learned is that *anger is a choice*. Our emotions do not control us. *We* control our actions; our emotions only have power over us if we allow them to overrule God's voice in our hearts. We have to choose to be calm instead of upset. We have to choose to be kind instead of cruel. We have to choose to be at peace rather than in turmoil.

As sad as it is, sometimes we want to hold on to our anger. Whether it's bitterness or the desire to take revenge doesn't matter. What matters is realizing we have to let it go and choosing to do so.

Ephesians 4:26 (NIV) warns, "In your anger do not sin: Do not the sun go down while you are still angry."

How many times have we laid down to sleep at night only to toss and turn because of some deep emotion in our hearts? How many times has this emotion been anger? The Bible warns us not to let the sun go down on our anger. That's because anger can lead to hatred, and hating others is a sin.

Whenever you're so upset that all you can see is red, remember that you can't let the sun go down on your anger. I don't care if it's not until the very moment before you fall asleep that you let go and choose joy and hope over sorrow and rage. I don't care if it's the first thing you do in the morning. All I care about is that you choose to let go of your anger. *This is a decision you have to make every day.*

Luke 9:23 (NKJV) says, "Then He said to them all, 'If anyone desires to come after Me, let him deny himself, and take up his cross daily, and follow Me.'"

However, starting off your morning with the decision to let go of anger, take up your cross, and follow Jesus will make your whole day so much better. Without this distraction, you will be so much more productive, kind, and loving. *When we are angry, it is extremely difficult, if not impossible, to show love to others as God would want us to.*

Don't let the sun go down on your anger. The sky may be dark but allowing anger to marinate in your heart is when true darkness will enter your life. How many parents have lashed out at their children for a small mistake after a hard day? How many teenagers have been so frustrated that they say something they really don't mean to an adult? How many times have friendships broken apart because they were too petty to talk out their differences? How many relationships have crumpled because one person is too angry or proud to have a real conversation with the other person after something happened?

If we choose to be angry—yes, it really is a choice—our lives will feel empty. We will constantly be exhausted, lacking energy and the motivation to do anything that doesn't have to do with our anger. When anger drives all our actions, we stop living the life God wants us to live and hand over the keys to Satan.

Satan wants you to be furious; *he wants to ruin your life*. He wants all your relationships to crash and burn, leaving you alone and hurting and broken. He wants you to give up on the Lord while you're raging about the bad things in your life. He wants you to curse God and live a life full of sin, a life that is cold and searing your very soul all at once. Satan wants you to be angry because choosing to be anything else seems too hard for you.

But, dear friends, 1 Corinthians 10:13 reminds us that there is no challenge we will meet which cannot be overcome with God on our side. When Satan tells us we are overwhelmed, God says He's got it all under control. When we tell ourselves we simply can't do it, God provides the courage and the words of forgiveness. When others tell us we should give up, God never stops reaching out to us with His warm, soothing embrace. Oddly enough, it's this tight embrace that gives us the room to let go of our anger.

Don't allow Satan to wreck your life, your relationships, and your dreams. Take the first step to overcoming your anger by choosing to let go.

2. The second part of overcoming your anger is pinpointing what made you upset in the first place.

God has given us the power to make good decisions and to choose how we act, no matter the situation and no matter the emotion. Maybe you're angry about your childhood, filled with abuse or injustice. Maybe you're angry about a past relationship, someone who cheated or didn't treat you right. Maybe you're holding a grudge against a friend who betrayed your secrets. Maybe you can't forget about a lie someone told you. Maybe your anger has stemmed from pride. When we feel disrespected or hurt, our hearts might become bitter. But we must stop ourselves from being bitter because it can lead to hatred. And hatred will tear your life apart. Maybe you're furious at God because of a loss in your family, a financial situation, or a rejection. When the blame starts to shift to God, we have to catch ourselves. We have to recognize that God is using our circumstances to draw us nearer to Him and to teach us how to forgive, letting go of all rage and bitterness, instead of falling into hate.

When we pinpoint the root of our anger, the source of the burning fire, and choose to see it as a gift from God to relate with others, learn forgiveness, and strengthen our faith, our world will be full of everlasting light; the seething bitterness we have clung to for so long will turn to ashes.

3. The third part of overcoming your anger is prayer.

Psalms 139:23-24 (NIV) pleads, "Search me, God, and know my heart; test me and know my anxious thoughts. See if there is any offensive way in me and lead me in the way everlasting."

Prayer is a sign to God that you have chosen to let go of your anger—you wouldn't be praying about it if you hadn't, even deep in your heart, decided to let go.

The amazing thing about prayer is that it doesn't just change our lives. It also changes the lives of others. People will see the change in your heart and be inspired to let go of anger as well. When people understand we've been exactly where they are, caught in the trap of anger, and have escaped, they will believe they can escape too. When we overcome anger, we can help others overcome anger through our own experiences and through prayer.

<u>4. The fourth part of overcoming your anger is looking at your situation through a new perspective and allowing it to positively change the way you act and feel.</u>

Prayer changes the way we view the world, and it can change the way we view situations or people that make us angry. *By praying to see people the way God sees them, we gain a deeper understanding and insight into who they are, which helps us to let go of our anger towards them.*

When I understood who I was and who I wanted to become, I was able to see life from a new point of view. Anger was not a part of who I wanted to become. So, I decided to let go of anger; I worked every day toward making this decision a reality.

When we pray for God to reveal sources of anger in our lives, He sends us on a life-long journey of forgiveness.

Friends, we can't become furious at every minor grievance, snide remark, and petty jibe. There is, however, a time for justified anger, a godly anger. This anger drives us to make good changes in our lives and in the world. It motivates us to pursue our dreams, and it seeks justice. But take caution: you need to learn the difference between godly anger and worldly anger to discern the right path.

Following these steps will help you live a life free from the burden of anger. Don't allow Satan to win—good things will never come of it.

When the sun goes down and we are angry, our hearts are not in the right place.

When the sun goes down and we are angry, forgiveness becomes harder every day.

When the sun goes down and we are angry, it becomes more difficult to let go and choose joy and hope.

When the sun goes down and we are angry, love is not within our grasp.

When the sun goes down and we are still angry, we have surrendered to Satan.

But, if we make the decision to let go of our anger, *beautiful* things will follow.

Psalms 113:3 (NKJV) says, "From the rising of the sun to its going down the Lord's name is to be praised."

If we choose to worship the Lord from when the sun comes up to when it goes down each and every day, our lives will be healthier, happier, and full of love. Rise from this place of anger and enter the place of constant praise to God. Enter into the wonderful hope and joy of the Lord.

If the sun goes down and we have chosen joy over hate, our lips will teem with never-ending praise.

If the sun goes down and we have chosen hope over holding grudges, all our interactions will overflow with the love of Jesus.

If the sun goes down and we have chosen everlasting light over darkness, our lives will overflow with blessings and the confidence that we can fight against the devil, and win, when we allow God to work in us.

Unwavering Focus

It is so easy to let distractions get in the way of serving God, but we have to choose to keep our eyes fixed on Jesus before we are ever even tempted to gaze at something else. When we make the decision to serve God during trials, our sight will remain fixed on His good and perfect light unerringly.

There are many stories in the Bible about people who kept their hearts and minds on Jesus and their eyes set heavenward. There are endless tales of Christians who were martyred, persecuted, or viciously beaten for their faith. However, today I want to share the humble story of a woman found in Matthew 26. We don't know the name of this woman, but we do know a very small part of her life and a very big part of her faith.

Right around the time when Judas agreed to betray Jesus for thirty pieces of silver, a woman had an encounter with Jesus at Bethany. She had an expensive flask of fragrant oil, something highly treasured at the time, something she was expected to save for an important event or urgent need.

But this woman did the exact opposite of what the world was telling her to do.

The world said she shouldn't waste the oil. The world told her she was wrong for pouring the oil on Jesus's precious head, which could have been sold and used for helping the poor. But God told her to anoint Jesus; she gladly said yes.

When the disciples ridiculed her, they didn't know she was helping to prepare Jesus for burial. When they questioned her, Jesus stepped in to defend her, to commend her faith. What happens next is amazing.

In Matthew 26:10-13 (NKJV), Jesus says, "… 'Why do you trouble the woman? For she has done a good work for Me. For you have the poor with you always, but Me you do not have always. For in pouring this fragrant oil on My body, she did it for my burial. Assuredly, I say to you, wherever this gospel is preached in the whole world, what this woman has done will also be told as a memorial to her.'"

Nothing is ever wasted on Jesus. In fact, that's where we should store all our most precious treasures.

This small act of obedience on the part of the woman, Jesus states, will now be remembered *forever*, wherever the Gospel is shared. One of the biggest parts of maintaining unwavering focus is obedience in things big and small. In her remarkable book *What Happens When Women Say Yes to God*, Lysa TerKeurst writes, "Even small acts of obedience have widespread effects."

I like to think of it like a ripple in a lake caused by a pebble. You throw the pebble into the water with a *plop,* and then rings of water disperse from the point of impact until the rings reach the edges of the lake.

In the same way, it only takes a small act of obedience or kindness or love to affect the world. By throwing your pebble into the lake, you intentionally choose to positively impact those around you with domino-effect results. When those around you see your unwavering focus on God and see you living a life full of sweet little pebbles, they will throw their pebbles in the water too, and so on, until the whole world is a mass of pebbles and ripples in a once still, quiet water.

All it takes is one person who decides to keep their unwavering focus on God, who chooses to take a leap of faith because they know God is with them. Like the story of the woman at Bethany, the smallest actions can lead to the greatest impacts.

She had unwavering focus on Jesus. She chose to rise from the place of disobedience and fear and timidity that Satan put her in and stepped into boldness, determination, and persistent obedience to please God.

When our focus is on Jesus, there is nothing we cannot do.

Philippians 4:13 (NKJV) encourages us, "I can do all things through Christ who strengths me."

Luke 1:37 (NKJV) emboldens us, "For with God nothing will be impossible."

Jeremiah 32:17 (ESV) declares, "Ah, Lord God! It is you who have made the heavens and the earth by your great power and by your outstretched arm! Nothing is too hard for you."

Job 42:2 (ESV) asserts, "I know that you can do all things, and that no purpose of yours can be thwarted."

And finally, Matthew 17:20 (ESV) says, "He said to them, 'Because of your little faith. For truly, I say to you, if you have faith like a grain of mustard seed, you will say to this mountain, 'Move from here to there.' and it will move and nothing will be impossible for you.'"

When we choose to keep our focus on God without fail, nothing will be impossible for us: God's power is limitless. Rise, let us turn away from our distractions and focus on God unwaveringly. No more setbacks. No more doubts. Turn away from the porn, the addictive technology, and the self-destructive behavior. Turn away from the overthinking and hopelessness and sorrow that cannot engulf you unless you let it. Turn away from the doubt, the insecurity, the fear of what others think. Turn away from sin and look to God. Rise, let us go from this place of temptations and distractions and keep our eyes on Jesus.

The woman was criticized by others for her godly, faith-filled actions when she poured the oil on the Savior's head, but Jesus made sure she would be remembered forever and shine everlasting light into the lives of all who read her story. Focus on Jesus, and the rest of the world will fall away until there are so many pebbles thrown into the water, so many ripples in the pond, that *there is no more room for Satan to work.*

Take Up Your Weapons: The Armor of God

As Christians, there are things and people in this world who will stop at nothing to thwart our goal: spreading the Good News. However, God has given us weapons to fight against the evil of this world.

Ephesians 6:10-18 (NIV) empowers us to fight on the Lord's behalf with the weapons He has provided for us, urging us, "Finally, be strong in the Lord and in his mighty power. Put on the full armor of God, so you can take your stand against the devil's schemes. For our struggle is not against flesh and blood, but against the rulers, against the authorities, against the powers of this dark world and against the spiritual forces of evil in the heavenly realms. Therefore, put on the full armor of God, so that when the day of evil comes, you may be able to stand your ground, and after you have done everything, to stand. Stand firm then, with the belt of truth buckled around your waist, with the breastplate of righteousness in place, and with your feet fitted with the readiness that comes from the gospel of peace. In addition to all this, take up the shield of faith, with which you can extinguish all the flaming arrows of the evil one. Take the helmet of salvation and the sword of the Spirit, which is the word of God. And pray in the Spirit on all occasions with all kinds of prayers and requests. With this in mind, be alert and always keep on praying for all the Lord's people."

God has given us these weapons to fight. There are two things we must choose to do. We must choose to take up our weapons; we must choose to fight. However, the world's version of fighting is much different from God's version. We must learn to use these weapons, yes, but we also have to let God fight for us. We must pray before, during, and after spiritual battles in order to succeed. Allowing God to fight for you simply means bringing your troubles to Him, asking for help, and allowing God to show you the way. All you have to do is choose. Will you take up your weapons through prayer and allow Jesus to fight for you, or will you allow Satan to win? Rise up from this place of apathy and pride and, with your godly weapons, stand to fight the good fight.

Remember that we are at war with the rulers who attempt to snuff out Christianity. We are struggling against all the evil in this dark world. We are grappling with the very darkness that seems to surround us. We aren't supposed to fight *against* God. We're supposed to fight *for* God. For our beliefs, our convictions, and our faith. We have to rise up. We have to take a stand. We have to take up our weapons. *And we have to put on the armor of God.*

Often, however, one of the greatest obstacles we must overcome to fight for the Lord is our own selfishness, unwillingness, or pain. Bad memories can be like an old battle wound. Whenever you think about or do something that triggers past trauma, all the darkness comes flooding back in and you drop your sword and become helpless. But this is the fact we must face today: those bad memories and experiences will not simply go away. Some things are nearly impossible to forget. But you can't live your life by completely trying to avoid pain. If you are constantly trying to avoid pain, you'll never experience relief. *To take up our weapons, we must rise from this place of fear and doubt and face whatever lies behind us. Only then can we fight against whatever comes before us.*

True Bravery

The six-day camps I attended in the summer, and the short weekend youth rallies, conferences, and retreats throughout the school year, all have a common attribute: the invitation. The invitation is a time when anyone who is lost or hurting can come up to the front of the auditorium and share their stories or ask for prayers. After I was sick in seventh grade, I placed my hope and my treasure in the light of all the wrong things, things that were not of Jesus. I wrestled with this for a long time, even while I was in godly places. There was something I knew I needed to do, and I was terrified to do it. I felt God calling me to go forward during the invitation, confess my sins and struggles, and ask for prayers. This was a terrifying thought because I often have a hard time being vulnerable with others. Going forward during the invitation is a very public thing.

As a child, I always marveled at the bravery of the people who slowly walked to the front, head bowed and face shiny with tears. To visibly see someone's grief and sorrow and regret breaks my heart. But each step they take towards the stage is a little lighter, as they near the time when they confess all they have done and choose to turn back to God.

They scribble what's on their hearts in shaky writing on a little notecard with their name scrawled at the top. They share their sins, struggles, and need for help and guidance in overcoming them. The invitation is intended to help people understand they can only find light and guidance through a committed relationship with God.

For each person who stands to walk forward alone, a group of family, friends, and fellow brothers and sisters in Christ file in behind them, right there with them the whole time. With God, no one walks alone.

After several minutes of people stepping up to pour their hearts out, a leader reads the notecards aloud. Written on the cards are stories about high schoolers who struggle with addiction, teenage moms, and children who were abused. They tell about good people who made bad decisions and people who have lost loved ones. They tell of sickness and anxiety and depression. A few cards even declare that someone wants to be baptized. Oh, what a beautiful day!

The leader prays over them. They walk back into the crowd lighter, with their friends hand in hand, because they chose to be baptized and will soon have the assurance of salvation through the sacrifice of Christ Jesus.

After the summer I turned back to God, I wanted so badly to share my story during an invitation. I had wanted to share what I was going through for a couple years before that too, but I never had the courage. I simply stayed in my seat and let the tears fall quietly, hoping nobody could see.

I used to think that needing help was weak, that leaning on others for support when I was stumbling somehow made me a burden. I did my best to hide my flaws and mistakes and trials. I should have talked to somebody, asked for advice, accepted an already extended hand. Instead, I chose to suffer in silence.

I knew my friends would be there in the blink of an eye if I called them. I knew my family would have done the same. Yet, I refused to seek help; I kept denying the action God was whispering to me to take.

The need to share my story kept growing and growing until I couldn't keep it in for a moment more. At a weekend youth rally, I walked to the front during the invitation for the first time.

As the invitation time began, I felt the ever-heavier weight on my heart yank me forward. In my head, I made excuses. I was wearing a Hawaiian shirt, and I didn't want to stand out to anyone, as I would already be boldly walking to the front. I didn't want people to wonder *Hey, that girl must have really messed up to be crying like that.* or *Huh, I know her. I wonder if she's okay.* I didn't want people to worry about me or look down on me for struggling. I questioned if my friends would really follow me up there, even though I was certain they would. The devil used all these silly excuses to sink doubt into my mind.

My eyes snapped up from where I had been looking at the floor as soon as I realized what Satan had been doing all along. He was trying to keep me from doing what God wanted for me. Satan liked watching me suffer alone, *savored* the feeling of my doubt and fear.

I closed my eyes briefly, preparing myself with a deep breath, and shuffled out of the row of closely positioned seats. I paused at the end of the aisle, still a little uncertain. I thought of how Satan had been tricking me, shoved him out of my mind, and allowed God's light to completely overwhelm my heart. *I took a step toward the stage.* Then another. And another.

I started out slow and stiff, but my stride soon became determined, humbled yet purposeful. Tears flowed freely down my face, but I held my head high, not caring if others saw my pain or what they thought of my tears. This was for me, a gift from God to lay down the burdens that held me back. And I was too thankful to be proud anymore.

I nodded to the man passing out notecards and pencils, and he offered a kind smile. When I sat down to write about my struggles and new-found determination, I looked up to see all my friends sitting down with me. Tears started falling anew, and I was reminded once again that God provides, and He provides abundantly.

While they held my hands, placed a hand on my shoulder, or embraced me, I was sad that I had pushed this moment away for so long. Now, I welcomed it.

I smiled at them through the tears. I was not alone. *None of us are alone.* They huddled around me as the leader read out all the cards and prayed. They cried with me.

When it was time to return to our seats, I walked light. I was no longer weighed down by the oppressive weight of loneliness and bottled-up emotions I had carried for so long. I was glowing with my newly discovered freedom. I felt God's presence as a hum of satisfaction and joy deep in my soul as the need to share my story abated. I felt Him cry with me; I knew He smiled with me, too.

Sometimes the greatest courage you can show is being vulnerable with someone by sharing your sufferings. God has given us these stories to spread His Word. Don't let your pain go to waste by ignoring God's whisper in your heart. Don't walk alone.

We must learn to be thankful for our flaws because they remind us that God is greater and grant us the opportunity to grow closer to Him and connect with those around us.

In 2 Corinthians, Paul explains that he was pierced by a "thorn in the flesh" (2 Corinthians 12:7 NKJV). We don't know what exactly this thorn in the flesh was, but we do know it was a struggle placed upon Paul so that he was humbled, and others would not overly praise him instead of God.

Paul pleaded with God to take away his thorn in the flesh three times, but God refused, answering, "My grace is sufficient for you, for my strength is made perfect in weakness." (2 Corinthians 12:9 NKJV)

Although it may have been difficult, Paul accepted what God said and then declared, "Therefore, most gladly I will rather boast in my infirmities, that the power of Christ may rest upon me. Therefore, I take pleasure in infirmities, in reproaches, in needs, in persecution, in distresses, for Christ's sake. For when I am weak, then I am strong." (2 Corinthians 12:10 NKJV)

When we are weakest in ourselves, we are strongest in God. Paul was thankful for his thorn in the flesh because it ultimately allowed the merciful love and mighty power of Christ to rest upon him. *He accepted God's answer and chose to be joyful even though he didn't receive the outcome he desired.* In a similar way, we should take pleasure in our sufferings and need for support, because when we confess what we are going through, God's presence will fill our souls with relief and comfort. Stop suffering in silence, listen to what God is telling you, and go confide in someone you can trust.

Paul also understood that we have to depend on each other in order for our faith to reach its full potential. In 1 Corinthians 12:26 (ESV) he writes, "If one member suffers, all suffer together; if one member is honored, all rejoice together."

We have to let others help us. We were made to suffer and rejoice *together*. We need love and comfort from our friends as much as we need God's light to guide our path. We will stand only if we stand *together*. Apart, we can accomplish nothing.

If we want to overcome the darkness of this world, we can't do it alone. But together, we will stand.

When we choose to walk hand in hand with our fellow Christians, God's everlasting light will shine through us stronger and brighter than it ever could have if we were working alone.

Ecclesiastes 4:12 (NLT) says, "A person standing alone can be attacked and defeated, but two can stand back to back and conquer. Three are even better, for a triple-braided chord is not easily broken."

Alone, a foe may be able to defeat us, but together no one can break us.

To live a life of everlasting light, we must be brave enough to be vulnerable with others. Choosing to stand alone is what really makes us weak. Admitting we need help and choosing to stand together is what makes us strong. God's strength is made perfect in our weakness. Rise and accept help. The strongest people are not afraid to be vulnerable with others. Remember that the next time Satan attempts to thwart God's will for you.

Gateway of Hope

I went on a prayer walk a couple of weeks ago, bringing before God a difficult past few days. The snow of the final thrust of winter melting, the sun shined upon the world in a bright yellow haze, the heat strange while piles of snow still frosted the street sides.

As I admired the antithesis of sun-warmed snow around me, I prayed. It seemed like everywhere I turned was a reminder of camp and traveling and all the places I couldn't go and all the things I couldn't do because of COVID. My heart ached. I missed it so much my chest felt pinched tight, and I could hardly breathe. In need of relief, I told God about how much I missed camp and traveling and Nicaragua.

"Lord, my heart is filled with all the places I want to go. It was so hard last year during the pandemic because I couldn't go anywhere. Not to summer camp or to travel around the world. Not to Nicaragua or anywhere else. I long for adventure, and I long to find You in new places, to see Your beautiful creation all over the earth. But God," my voice broke,

"I'm hurting and I'm struggling and I'm tired." A tear slipped down my cheek. "I don't know what to do. I've been waiting for so long and I'm growing impatient. But God, I choose to wait on You, however long it takes, because I trust in You."

I walked along in silence for a bit, tears clouding my vision. In my head, though, I prayed for God to allow me to travel and go to camp this year. It was coming up soon, and I was worried it would be canceled. But even if I didn't get to go, I promised God I would still love and trust Him and His plan, because it is always better than anything I ever could have laid out.

As I continued to pray, God called to mind a certain verse I read a couple months prior. In Hosea 2:15 (NLT) God promises, "I will return her vineyards to her and transform the Valley of Trouble into a gateway of hope."

Immediately, I realized why my heart was so heavy. I was not hoping in the Lord alone—I wasn't even hoping that I could receive what I prayed for in this situation. Yes, I longed to go to camp and to travel, but I wasn't yet hoping for it. The truth is, I was afraid.

After being told no so many times last year, my heart grew wary of hoping. Every time I was let down, I turned to God, and He reminded me not to place my hope in anything but Him. "When your hopes are placed in Me alone, Lily," He reminded me, "you will never be disappointed."

This realization stopped me in my tracks on my sunset prayer walk. I knew what I had to do. If I wanted God to answer any of my prayers, I had to dare to hope.

During quarantine, I learned so much about how to hope. However, several months had passed, and I was used to things being open again. So, when I was presented with a challenge that required a lot of hope, I realized I had forgotten how.

In a book called *Daring to Hope: Finding God's Goodness in the Broken and the Beautiful,* a book that changed my life, Katie Davis Majors says,

"It is a brave thing to hope, to continue to hope, knowing God might say yes but that He could say no, and choosing to hope anyway."

Longing is not the same thing as hoping. Yes, I longed for camp and travel, but I wasn't hoping for it. In a way, I was trying to guard my heart against pain by never letting myself hope in the first place. *This is the worst thing we can do as Christians when we are afraid.*

We have to choose to hope no matter what. And when we do gather the courage to hope, God will either say yes or no, but either way, as long as our hope is based in our Savior, His answer will only draw us nearer to Him.

So, I stood there in the middle of the street and took the first step towards learning to hope again: I asked for forgiveness. And after I asked for forgiveness, I softened my heart, allowed the walls I had built around me to crumble, and chose to hope.

A smile broke across my face even as tears filled my eyes, reminding me of the sun and the snow. This time as I spoke with God, my words and requests were deeply rooted in the hope of the Savior, even though it meant breaking my heart to see His light.

As I walked, I prayed for inspiration for writing. I thought of all the books I longed to write and adventures I dreamed about. I hoped and believed, for these two things are inextricably intertwined, that God would provide.

In quarantine, I learned how to only hope in God and not in what He could do for me or in my circumstances or worldly wishes. My hope only belongs in God, the one true hope. I had to remind myself of this, and I told God that I was willing to wait patiently for his plan no matter how long it took. Wherever He wanted me to go, whenever He wanted me to go there, I would listen. *I walked through the Gateway of Hope.*

What the Lord says in Hosea 2:15 is true. God turns the Valley of Trouble into a Gateway of Hope. He turns the darkness in our lives into joy by shining hope, a crucial piece of His everlasting light, upon us. At night, it can be hard to see what's right in front of you, but when there's light, you won't fear what lies ahead. I learned to be thankful for the darkness and the pain I was experiencing because God turns our trials and fears into opportunities to grow closer to Him.

When I chose to walk through the Gateway of Hope, not in spite of my fear, but because I decided to overcome it, my life was filled with God in a beautiful overflow of blessings and love and answered dreams, all because I took an opportunity He placed before me to strengthen my relationship with Him. *When we walk through the Gateway of Hope, God provides.*

Later that same night, God answered so many prayers all at once. I was offered the chance to travel with a group to Paris, Venice, and Switzerland in the upcoming summer. And there was somehow one spot left just for me.

I couldn't believe it at first. I was shocked and I started crying. God provided. When we walk through the Gateway of Hope, completely placing our hope in God, He begins to answer our prayers and desires, even the ones we never dreamed of receiving but dared to hope might be gifted to us.

After my mom and my aunt told me the news, I called to ask my dad about going. He said yes but reminded me to always thank God.

Dreams can come true, but you must choose to walk through the Gateway of Hope, a door with many barriers to entering in our own hearts, to achieve them. Although there are obstacles such as fear or pain or doubt in our hearts, we can't allow this to prevent us from hoping in God. *We have to choose to hope not in spite of these barriers, but because going through them is the only way we will ever reach the Gateway of Hope.* Through this beautiful gate, past all these obstacles, is a beautiful place of everlasting light and answered prayers.

On top of providing me a chance to travel, I got to spend time talking about my trip with my best friend, who was so happy for me. As the weather warmed up, I got to read outside, taking in all God's creation. I found out that the team did really well for the state competition of

Academic Decathlon. I had some delicious chocolate, and if you know me at all, you know how much I love chocolate. This chapter is even an answered prayer as I asked God to help me finish this book and provide the experiences and wisdom for what I wanted to write about.

In the darkness and the light that came through and after it, Psalm 30:5 (NKJV) came true once again, reminding me, "Weeping may endure for a night, but joy comes in the morning."

Walking through the Gateway of Hope when our lives are so dark we can't even find the path will lead to greater joy than we can ever imagine. I had forgotten what the joy of traveling felt like, the period of excitement leading up to the moment you hop on a plane, the anticipation of adventures the trip might hold. I thanked God every day for this joy and remembered what my dad said. I would not forget to thank God.

My choice to hope patiently, no matter how much it hurt or how hard it was, was rewarded. As I practiced my French and Italian for the upcoming trip, I learned something fascinating. The word "day" in French is "journée." I absolutely love this. Every day we have to make the journey to the Gateway of Hope and choose to walk through it. We can't walk through the Gateway of Hope if we don't first make the journey there. What does this journey look like for you? For me, it took the pandemic and everything being canceled to learn to dare to hope in God and Him alone, not to be sure of uncertain circumstances or wish for things that aren't what God wants.

Every day's journey looks a little different, but everyone has a daily journey to choose hope and joy. Sometimes it happens as soon as our eyes pop open; sometimes it doesn't happen until the moment before we fall asleep. All that matters is that it *does* happen.

I had been struggling to feel God near, but when I chose to walk through the Gateway of Hope, I was overjoyed in a way I hadn't been in a long time. I was able to reconnect with my daily Bible reading after struggling to find deeper connection for a while. I was able to write with more passion. I was able to show more love to others.

When I realized I had been struggling to feel God, I turned to Him in prayer and asked Him to reveal His presence and give me opportunities to serve Him. He provided abundantly.

A few days after I found out that I was going to Europe, I got to attend camp for the first time in over a year, for the first time since quarantine last spring. From the weeks leading up to it to the night before we planned to leave, I was terrified it would be just another thing that got canceled. I was struggling to hope big time, but through prayer and God's kind and gentle help, I was able to step through the Gateway of Hope. I hoped I would get to go to camp and feel God's presence in the way I longed for so much. I hoped I would get to see some old friends I hadn't seen in so long. I hoped for fun and relaxation and opportunities to be a light.

Although all these things are good, I realized yet again I was hoping in things other than God alone. As I was on my sunset prayer walk, I recognized this and talked to God about it. I knew He understood, and by the time I returned to my house, I was right with God, and my hope was refocused. *Instead of hoping in what God can do for us, we just need to hope in Him.*

When I stopped hoping in what He could do and started placing my trust in Him during quarantine, my whole perspective of life changed. I no longer saw events being canceled as a sad occasion but as a reason to praise God for the opportunity to grow closer to Him. However, a year had passed, and I grew accustomed to things no longer being canceled. I lost sight of where my hope should be placed and struggled to focus on God again. Dear friends, we can't forget the lessons we have learned throughout our lives, no matter how much time has passed. We have to remember what we have learned so we can abide by it forever and live the satisfying, joy-filled life God intended for us.

The night before camp, I poured my heart out to God. I told Him how excited I was. I told Him that no matter what happened, I would trust in Him, even if it hurt in the end, even if it felt nearly impossible, because I knew He had the best plan for me. Trust is a decision. Sometimes, instead of simply walking through the Gateway of Hope, we have to take a leap of faith to cross its threshold. And leap I did.

I fell asleep that night, content and peaceful because I made the decision to trust God no matter what happened. If I finally got to go to camp this time, I chose to praise and thank Him. But if I didn't, I chose to love Him and bring glory to Him all the same.

I woke up the next morning smiling. The moment I hopped on the bus to drive to Gatlinburg felt a lot like stepping through the Gateway of Hope. When we place our hope in God alone, our hopes are always answered: God never fails.

That weekend was one of the best experiences I've ever had with camp and with learning to hope in a new way. It seemed like every prayer of what this weekend would be, every small hope and desire of my heart I hadn't even voiced to God, was fulfilled. When we walk through the Gateway of Hope into the trust and peace and love that abounds on the other side, God places opportunities in front of us to bring glory to His name through our belief.

One of these wonderful opportunities occurred on the church van as we played games, ate snacks, and talked to kill time. At one point, the topic of conversation turned to baptism. My friend Sarah Grace shared how she had wanted to be baptized but was scared. She felt like she didn't deserve to be baptized because of the way she had treated others and seemed to come off as mean or rude when she was just trying to be a little sassy.

I dared to hope that God would give me the opportunity to bring glory to Him by helping a lost soul back into His arms. I prayed and released the situation into His capable hands. God provided me with the wisdom, courage, and words to guide her.

Later that night, I had the opportunity to talk to Sarah Grace more. I explained that we all mess up and we've all done bad things, but it's not about us. It's about God. Baptism isn't about how worthy we are. It's about Jesus sacrificing Himself on the cross so we could be forgiven and have the hope of God in heaven and live our lives in a way that brings honor to Him. *Baptism is a decision we make when we want to stop living in sin and start living in everlasting light.*

After listening and talking to Sarah Grace and determining that she wanted to get baptized for the right reasons, we talked to the youth minister, and she was baptized in the cabin's indoor pool later that same night.

My heart was overjoyed that God gave me this opportunity to play a small part in the saving of a kind, beautiful soul. My hopes were fulfilled. My entire being was glad to gain a new sister in Christ. I prayed and God provided. As amazing as this was, God was far from done working. I prayed, and He provided even more abundantly.

Another friend in the youth group sat with us as we talked about baptism. She shared how she had wanted to get baptized for the past several months. Her mom approved; she wanted to be baptized for the right reasons. There was only one thing standing in her way: her dad kept telling her she wasn't ready.

As she shared her story with me, I learned that her dad got upset often, and a sure way for her to anger him was to disobey him by getting baptized. She was afraid to be baptized because she didn't want her dad to get offended.

As much as it broke my heart to hear this, I explained that nobody could make this decision but her. Nobody can tell you when it's time to get baptized. That's a decision you have to make for yourself. When the time is right, you will know it in your heart. Her dad continually telling her she wasn't ready when she was, was Satan attempting to get in the way of her getting to heaven. *The decision to be baptized and save your soul is a decision you have to make no matter what is going on around you.*

After talking and praying together, I went to my room, got onto my knees by the couch, and prayed for God to soften the heart of her dad so she could be baptized without fear. A few short minutes later, she came to me with the biggest smile on her face after receiving a text from her mom. She told me that her dad said it was okay for her to get baptized. We were so joyful we couldn't help but laugh and thank God for answering our prayers. (After so long of waiting for some prayers to be answered, it was amazing to watch God work quickly right before my eyes.)

She was baptized soon after; our joy was made complete. When God provides, He provides abundantly. When we choose to hope in God with all we have, jumping through the Gateway of Hope instead of sticking the tip of our pinky toe through the door, He will respond in kind. God rewards great faith and hope and love. One day, we will receive this reward in heaven, but while we are here on earth, this reward comes in the form of opportunities and blessings that bring us joy. Sometimes this reward will even come through trials.

A couple days after we returned home, my sophomore class was required to take the ACT. We arrived at school and reported to our classrooms by 7:15 a.m. to start testing. Well, we were supposed to anyway. The school sent out the wrong information, so several people couldn't find the right testing rooms. Once they got everything sorted out, we were already twenty minutes behind schedule. Then the intercom started making this horrible screeching noise that didn't stop for at least ten minutes. When we were thirty minutes behind, we started filling out the personal and required information on the front of the answer document. This took over an hour because there were more questions than anyone had realized or planned for. So we started the actual test after almost two hours of setbacks and complications.

In spite of all these difficulties, I felt more confident than I ever had about the test when I finished about three hours later. I drove home feeling good, but when I turned into my garage, I took the turn a bit too sharp and scraped Baby, my car, all down the driver's side. I was frustrated with myself because I kept making mistakes even when I was trying to be so careful. My parents were surprisingly understanding and forgiving, and I am so thankful for that. I could have chosen to complain about how terrible taking the test was or how I scraped Baby, but instead I chose to focus on how God allowed me to do well on the test and how forgiving and kind my parents were.

Oftentimes our most stressful and sorrowful seasons can also be our most joyful. How can such joy and sorrow exist simultaneously? Well, it's all because of hope. Hope not in spite of sorrow, but because of the joy that will shine through the darkness into our hearts and lives.

Isaiah 53:3 (NKJV) states, "He is despised and rejected by men, a Man of sorrows and acquainted with grief. And we hid, as it were, our faces from Him; He was despised, and we did not esteem Him."

Jesus was a man of sorrows who had the greatest joy and suffering of all—to be sacrificed on the cross so we might live and return to the Father in heaven. Although the cross was horrifically painful to endure, Jesus did not despise the shame because of the hope He had for us. *This hope is what brought Him joy in the worst moments of His life.*

As He was beaten and forced to carry the cross on his bloody, shredded back to the place where He was nailed to it, imagine His pain. Every muscle screaming in agony, every human instinct telling Him to give up and fall down and stay there. But Jesus did not die on the way to Golgotha, the Place of the Skull. He died after He was nailed to the cross, forced to drag Himself up with all His strength to take a breath. And yet, He regarded His persecutors and tormentors with no ill will. Crying out to God in Luke 23:34 (NKJV), Jesus says, "Father, forgive them, for they do not know what they do." Imagine the sorrow and pain Jesus must have been feeling—physical, spiritual, mental, and emotional. And yet it's because of this pain that He was able to find joy. He knew that His pain would heal us. His sacrifice would make us whole. His death would give us life. He dared to hope that through His suffering, we would repent and learn to hope in Him.

Imagine this hope He must have felt on the cross, hope that we might follow Him. Are you living in a way that proves Jesus' sacrifice was not in vain? Have His hopes been answered in your life, in your heart? Or is He disappointed again and again by your refusal of hope, lack of belief, or failure to trust in Him? Jesus stepped through the Gateway of Hope. It's time we join Him on the other side.

When we hope in God, we are never really let down because God never lets us down. It's when we place our hope in anything else, even things that seem good, that makes us doubt in God when our wishes don't come true.

As it turns out, the trip to Europe got canceled. Although I was disappointed and sad, it was actually a blessing in disguise. After I found out, I decided to take a sunset prayer walk—I felt God calling me to chase the sunset and seek the Lord. As I walked, I talked to Him about how I was feeling and started naming all the many blessings in my life at the moment.

The world was blooming, so I picked a small handful of wild daisies from the side of the road. *It's always easier to think with a flower in your hand.* It makes the world seem sweeter, brighter somehow, amidst the chaos. There's just something about holding an object God so tenderly created for our amazement close to my heart as I pray and think that makes me feel connected to God through His beautiful creation.

In addition to the wonderful springtime blossoms, I got to laugh the day away with my friends at school, riding a scooter down the halls for a commercial I was filming in speech class. I did well at my Academic Decathlon competition, and the team was heading to Nationals! My little brother said his very first prayer after months of saying prayers and singing to him before he fell asleep. God answers prayers, and the hopes that surface in our hearts, if we wait patiently and trust Him through the journey day by day.

As I neared the top of a hill, I closed my eyes and took a deep breath. I chose to hope (in God alone), and I chose to be joyful, even though my heart was broken, because I believed God would provide abundantly if I waited patiently.

I opened my eyes and traveled the next few feet to the top of the hill. I turned around and grinned at the sunset before me. I breathed it all in and wished on a dandelion that I could hold this sunset, this hope, this joy, in my heart's memory forever. To me, the Gateway of Hope looks a lot like waiting patiently with a flower tucked behind my ear, staring at the wonders of God all around me, and watching everything turn to gold as the sun disappears to reveal the stars, preparing the world for a new day.

Sometimes it takes sorrowful situations to draw out the joy inside us, waiting for the time to dawn and shine upon our lives like the hope of a new morning. Everlasting light is on the other side of the Gateway of Hope. Joy is coming after the night of sorrow. All we have to do is choose to step through by hoping in God alone and the darkness can never touch or overwhelm us again.

Remember: Turning on the Light

In her famous book series *Harry Potter*, J.K. Rowling writes, "Happiness can be found, even in the darkest of times, if one only remembers to turn on the light."

When we're in the middle of trials, it is so easy to give up, and the temptation is great. But God doesn't want us to give up. There is a purpose for the night you are walking through, and one of those purposes is for God to teach you to remember.

Psalm 119:55 (ESV) says, "I remember your name in the night, O Lord, and keep your law."

If you want to live a life of everlasting light, you must remember *who* your everlasting light is and all the good He has done. The Israelites continually forgot the Lord and were consumed with complaining. They complained about being hungry and thirsty, and when God provided food, they complained it wasn't the kind of food they wanted. They complained about their leader, Moses, whom God appointed, and worshipped idols. They even complained that God was asking too much of them.

The Israelites were consumed with complaining even though God performed miracle after miracle to remind them of His presence. When they couldn't cross the Red Sea, God parted the waters. When they were thirsty, God made water flow from a rock. When they were hungry, God sent manna and quail. God appeared as a pillar of cloud by day and a pillar of fire by night to guide the Israelites' way. He made sure they never grew tired while traveling; their clothes never tore. God provided and took care of them, and all they did was complain. He gave them every reason to flip the switch, yet they still refused to turn on the light.

When the Israelites complained, Moses rebuked them, saying, "Then take care lest you forget the Lord, who brought you out of the land of Egypt, out of the house of slavery." (Deuteronomy 6:12 ESV)

Part of flipping the switch into a life of everlasting light is keeping God's commands when the night is long and hard. The Israelites spent forty years in the wilderness on their journey to the Promised Land. Revealing why God sent them along this path. Deuteronomy 8:2 (NIV) says, "Remember how the Lord your God led you all the way in the wilderness these forty years, to humble and test you in order to know what was in your heart, whether or not you would keep his commands."

The same thing happened with Abraham. God told Abraham to sacrifice his only son as a test of his faithfulness, and Abraham was willing to do what God asked no matter what. Because of his obedience, God sent an angel to stop him from sacrificing Isaac. *God sends tests and trials to determine the state of our heart, if we love God and are willing to follow Him at any cost, and to put our faith into action by remembering to keep His commands in all circumstances.*

Joseph suffered greatly at the hands of his brothers who, consumed with jealousy, sold Joseph into slavery. Yet through all this, he remained obedient, and God helped him prosper. When he was thrown into prison for a crime he didn't commit, he became the keeper of the prison. Through his God-given ability to interpret dreams, he was freed from prison and became second only to Pharaoh in the land of Egypt. God put Joseph in the position to save people all over the world when a famine struck the earth. Even his brothers, who so envied him at first, bowed before the glory of God shining through him many years later. Some people are meant to lead, and God will use these people to bring glory to Him. But God doesn't just want great leaders and famous people and politicians. He wants you and me, and all He asks for before He uses us to accomplish His will is that we remember to turn on the light. That's something anyone can do. *We don't have to be perfect.* Joseph started out as arrogant; God humbled him to use him for His purpose. All you have to do is make the choice like Joseph to serve God no matter where you are in life, and He will lift you up. Genesis 50:19-21 (NKJV) reads, "Joseph said to them, 'Do not be afraid, for am I in the place of God? But as for you, you meant evil against me; but God meant it for good, in order to save many people alive. Now therefore, do not be afraid; I will provide for you and your little ones.' And he comforted them and spoke kindly to them."

God sends trials for a reason, and often it's those challenges that have the greatest impact on our lives and the lives of those we cross paths with. It's beautiful to see how God uses the events in our lives for His glory and our sufferings to bring others closer to Him. It confounds me that God can take my body image problems, past illnesses, and current struggles and turn them into an opportunity to learn confidence and to be a light to others grappling with the same thing.

2 Peter 1:12 (NCV) promises, "You know these things, and you are very strong in the truth, but I will always help you remember them."

Every time I look in the mirror, I am reminded of God's voice, and I remember who I am and who He made me to be. Through this, and all my other struggles, trials, and triumphs, God taught me how to turn on the light in all circumstances. He taught me to be hopeful and to follow Him in big and small ways day by day. He taught me to be thankful for what I have and to love others around me the way Jesus did. He taught me what everlasting light looks like and how to live life to the full. But most of all, He taught me to remember to be joyful in dark times. He taught me how to look back on all the wonder-filled moments in my life and draw my strength from the eternal source of all peace and patience and goodness that never runs dry. He taught me that He answers prayers and that He is good no matter what. He taught me to say yes to His tap on my heart and to be a willing servant. He taught me how to use my gifts to bring glory to Him and how to inspire others to share their gifts and stories. He taught me to be patient and to live a life of interruptions and to take every opportunity presented to me. He taught me not to be afraid. He taught me to be confident and kind and humble. He taught me to be a friend. He taught me to trust that He will always provide.

In a lot of ways, I wrote this book selfishly. Not only is it intended to help others seek and find everlasting light in their lives, but it's intended to help me look back and remember all God has done for me.

I have found that when I am anxious, nothing calms my heart like remembering. Instead of focusing on what lies ahead and worrying about what might happen, I think about all the past times God has delivered me and choose to have confidence that He will carry me through again. Instead of questioning if God is real or if He will truly work in my life, I look back on the times I've heard His soft whisper, felt Him gently tapping on my heart, or experienced His love in amazing ways. Instead of being sorrowful, hopeless, or anxious, I choose to focus on God and say yes to the opportunities He places in front of me.

There have been many nights when I couldn't sleep. I tossed and turned, relentlessly uncomfortable and too nervous to stay still. I would lay in bed for hours trying to fall asleep, anxious about an upcoming test or soccer tryouts or simply whatever I may have to face the next day. I tried every trick in the book to get some shut-eye. Counting sheep, taking nighttime vitamins, and doing yoga didn't help on the worst nights. When I began to understand I couldn't do this by my own power, I prayed and asked God to help me. When I turned to Him humble and helpless, He provided every time.

When you can't sleep, don't entirely rely on human techniques to calm your heart and mind. Turn to God in prayer and choose to praise Him no matter what. If you rely on yourself you will never succeed, but if you rely on God's strength, power, and wisdom you will always claim the victory in the end.

Lights-out singing is one of my favorite things about camp: everything else in the world fading to black as God becomes the only light shining through our praise. During quarantine, when camp was canceled, one of the things I missed most was raising my voice to God in song side by side with my friends. But just because I couldn't be at camp with my friends and have lights-out singing didn't mean I couldn't have lights-out singing at all.

On the nights I couldn't sleep, feeling overwhelmed and stressed, I turned off all the lights in my room, sat on the floor by my bed, and sang, turning on the light in my heart. I sang as tears fell down my cheeks and as my words wobbled with emotion. I sang even when my voice broke. I sang until my sorrow became peace. I sang until my anxiety became joy. I sang until my helplessness became God's strength. I sang until my defeat became hope in Jesus. I sang until my doubt and fear became confidence that the Lord would provide.

I sang until I did not feel alone anymore, remembering the feel of my friends' hands in mine, standing to serve the Lord together. Though they weren't there in the flesh, they were there in spirit, and that was more than enough to comfort my heart.

When my tears were dried and my heart was stilled, I would flip onto my knees and say a prayer, completely releasing control to God and surrendering to Him. Most nights, I quickly fall asleep after my mini lights-out singing, but some nights it takes a little longer for God to calm my mind. If I'm finally able to sleep at peace, I choose to love Him. If I'm still unable to sleep, I choose to love Him. *We have to make the decision to love God, not in spite of what we may face, but because of what we will face. We have to love God at all times, because at all times we need Him.*

Don't turn to God only in your times of need. Turn to Him each and every day, each and every night before you try to sleep, regardless of whether you're restless or not. If your mind is at ease, praise Him for giving you peace. If you are joyful, praise Him for your success. If you are weary, ask Him to give you true rest in Him. If you are anxious, ask Him to help you remember.

Every night before I go to sleep, regardless of whether or not I'm worried, I pray, "Dear God, thank You for everything You've given me. Please help everyone to have a deep and replenishing sleep to prepare them for the day tomorrow. Please give me sweet dreams and calm my mind and heart so I might rest peacefully. Help me to love everybody always and to be a light to all those I come in contact with. Protect me from sickness and continually heal me. I remember Your past deeds and I trust You, God, because I know and believe You have taken care of me in the past and You will provide in the present and the future. Amen."

For a long time, this was my nightly prayer. That is, until I read a devotional about overcoming your fears. My cry out to God changed. I didn't pray for God to protect me from sickness, but I prayed for God to help me overcome my fears, even if it meant facing it head-on. Even if it meant getting sick again. I prayed for God to help me remember He would be with me so I could turn on the light and allow my fear to dissipate.

The next morning, I woke up and didn't feel well. God had answered my prayer. I didn't pray to get sick, but I did pray to overcome my fears; I knew sickness might have to be a part of that. I still prayed because I knew it was what God wanted me to do. He was giving me the opportunity to face my fear and overcome it, this time turning to Him and trusting in Him all the way through.

As I walked and prayed the next day, I noticed a shape in the clouds. It seemed there were two eye-shaped clouds on the horizon, one closed and one wide open. It appeared that God was winking at me. I turned to my heart to see what God was trying to say. It seemed He was telling me my prayer was answered, more than one prayer, actually. This would help me conquer my fear of sickness and provide the perfect ending for my first book. I accepted the trial with joy and decided to do being sick right this time. I prayed; I chose joy before I even knew what I was going to face, something I try to do not only during big trials, but also every morning before I start my day. I decided to follow God all the way through whatever was coming my way. And He provided.

Everlasting light shined in my life through the sickness, setting me free from worry. *It all started with choosing joy because of my God, not in spite of my circumstances.*

I asked for God to reveal if this was the right direction. Surely enough, the night stars were winking at me too, as was the eyelash of the crescent moon. "You do have a sense of humor don't You, God?" I said to myself, tapping my chin with my index finger. "Well, I guess I do love to laugh." I grinned, chuckling to myself.

Nevertheless, even though we think we know the path we might be headed down, 1 Corinthians 2:11 (NIV) reminds us, "… no one knows the thoughts of God except the Spirit of God."

I was tired and didn't feel well for a couple days; I expected to come down with some type of sickness, maybe even COVID-19 or even the flu and pneumonia again. However, I rested and spent some time in the sun and in prayer, and I was well. I never really got super sick, but I also never prayed for God to prevent me from getting sick. I prayed for His will of conquering my fears to be achieved by whatever means He desired so I could better serve Him. God knew my heart was in the right place, and I didn't have to get the flu or pneumonia again to learn this: *God's everlasting light will break through your dark cloud of fear to reveal a brighter side to every situation. You just have to remember to turn on the light.*

Epilogue:
We've Still Got It

On May 30, 2021, I stepped onto the bus to go to my first week-long church camp in two years. Throughout the whole pandemic, I thought this day would never come. But it finally did.

Not only was that week at camp one of the best weeks of camp in my life, but it was also one of the most empowering, inspiring, and strengthening. The theme? We've Still Got It.

The theme came from a song that talks about how after everything we've gone through, we still have joy, hope, love, faith, and peace. Even after the pandemic, canceled events, and quarantine, we still have all the good things God has gifted to us. I hope that over the course of this book you have chosen God above all things and made Him Lord of your life.

Although this was an amazing week at camp, there was one thing that made it really hard to have fun and stay positive. On Tuesday, all the older kids from my church were called to talk to the counselors. A few days earlier, we had heard the news that a girl who used to be in our youth group, Patti, had gone missing. The next day, we heard that they found her car abandoned and full of blood, then they told us that Patti had been brutally murdered by a man over a fight that began at a gas station.

We were all in tears and didn't know how to feel or what to do. We did our best to comfort one another and remember to trust in God. It was hard at first, but as the week progressed we found rest in His arms.

One night, a man spoke about magical moments in our lives, moments when we experience God in seemingly small yet incredible ways. There were so many magical moments and conversations, even during this great sorrow, that I can't include them all, but I want to share my favorite.

On the last night of camp, my counselor took a group of friends and I to watch the sunset on the dock over the lake. When we stepped into a clear view of the sky, it took my breath away. The sky, light blue and gentle, reflected gold and pink onto the waters, reminding me of tender morning light sent to wake you up in the morning. After a fairly rainy week without any colorful sunsets, this seemed to be God saying, "Lily, I will always take care of you. I will always provide for you abundantly. Trust in me, and I will give you exactly what you need."

Tears started to roll down my cheeks, and I just stood there and thanked God for a magical week at camp, exactly how I had hoped it would be. It wasn't magical in spite of the sorrow and death—it was magical because it drew my friends and I that much nearer to God. All my waiting and growing and longing was not in vain. My patience paid off. Camp was everything I hoped and dreamed and prayed it would be. It was even more than that. It was fulfilling and encouraging and thought-provoking. It was exactly what I needed: It was joy. It was light. It was a reminder to hope and remember God is good and He will provide.

After seeing the sunset, I gave a devotional to the girls in my cabin. I read one of the first chapters of my book, "Chasing Sunsets and Seeking the Lord." Everyone was in tears. It was the perfect ending to a wonderful week at camp.

Although some pretty rough stuff happened, it all reminded me that great joy and great sorrow can exist simultaneously because of hope. And that after all we've been through, we've still got everlasting light.

Acknowledgments

Thank you to all the friends and family who allowed me to use their stories and who helped me to publish *Everlasting Light*. Kack, Barry, Matt, Jeannie, Nana, Bob, Grandma Cherry, Pop Pop, Gigi, my parents, and so many others, your lives are a part of this book as much as mine. I thank you for allowing me to share this special connection with you.

Thank you, Madison Griffin, for the amazing author photos! Your creativity amazes me. You are a great friend; I'm glad to have you in my life.

Taylor Roberson. What can I even say? YOU ARE SO TALENTED!! Without your cover art, this book would never have lived up to all I dreamed it would be. Thanks to you, it did. I love you so, so much and I'm so proud of you. I can't wait to work with you more in the future!

A big thanks to Treava, who helped me with one of the original rough drafts of my book and who constantly inspires and encourages me. I admire your faith, joy, and love for God.

Pop Pop, without you I never would have published this book. I thank God for you often.

Thank you, Betty Ann and Coy Hathcock, for showing me how to glorify God in impossibly dark situations where there seems to be no light shining at all. I will never forget the importance of having a godly man in my life, and I will never forget Patti. She is a blessing. I admire your courage and strength. I love both of you and your beautiful, willing hearts so much. God is with you.

Thank you to my parents, who put up with my writing all the time and supported and encouraged me all the way through.

Thank you to the people who keep me in check, especially my fantastic teachers: Mrs. Billingsley, Ms. Mullins, Dr. Coffman, Mr. Young, Mr. Clark, Mrs. Soriano, Mr. Taylor, and so many others. You know who you are.

Thank you, Hannah, for being a wonderful friend and for making my world brighter. Never stop smiling and never give up. You are so, so beautiful.

Thank you, Molly Plyler, for your comforting words and for sharing a piece of your story when I was overwhelmed with grief and sadness the week of Patti's death. Even though you didn't know it, you said just the right thing.

Thank you, Seth, for always listening to the rough draft of whatever I'm working on and helping me to be a better person and a better writer. I love you, *babe*.

Thank you, Kalyn Stratton, for helping me figure out the signature I wanted to use to sign my books. You are very dear to my heart.

Aaron, thank you for appreciating my bad melodramatic poetry. And thank you for writing "Pepper the Cat." It is one of the greatest poems in existence.

Thank you, Abbie Kyridakidis, for being one of my favorite camp friends ever! I will be praying for you, and I know you are going to do beautiful things with your writing. Thanks for talking to and encouraging me.

Thank you, Brad, for camp. And thank you for being unafraid to share your magical ideas with the world. You make earth a better place.

Thank you, Justin and Savannah Smith, for being the first to take my youth group to camp. You have changed all of our lives for Jesus.

Thank you to my camp peeps, Holly (my tooth fairy), Addison, Maggie, Hailey, and the rest of the Gogurt Gang, as well as Emma (my camp mom), Brea, Miles, Roxie, Hadley, Emily, Mia, Taylor, and the Beetlebum cabin, for being some of the first groups of people to hear a chapter of my book. And thank you for encouraging me to keep writing with your kind words and deep insights. Never stop growing. I love you guys so much.

A big shoutout to the Westbow Press team for making this process smooth and for all your encouragement. You guys are wonderful!

And most of all, I thank God for all the wonders He has performed in my life and the lives of others. I don't know who or where I would be without Him, and so I thank Him for the gift of life to the full and hope to show others how they can find it, too. Amen.

Made in the USA
Columbia, SC
28 April 2023

15878135R00157